INVITING
PORCHES

210 Home Plans
with Perfect Porches

HOME PLANNERS, LLC
Wholly owned by Hanley-Wood, LLC

Published by Home Planners, LLC
Wholly owned by Hanley-Wood, LLC

Editorial and Corporate Offices:
3275 W. Ina Road, Suite 110
Tucson, Arizona 85741

Distribution Center:
29333 Lorie Lane
Wixom, Michigan 48393

President: Jayne Fenton
Executive Editor: Linda B. Bellamy
Editorial Director: Arlen Feldwick-Jones
Managing Editor: Vicki Frank
Associate Editor: Kristin Schneidler
Plans Associates: Tina Grijalva, Jennifer Lowry
Graphic Designer: Teralyn Morriss
Senior Production Manager: Sara Lisa
Production Manager: Brenda McClary

Photo Credits:

Front cover: Plan HPT740024, see page 32. Design ©William Poole Designs, Inc.,
photograph by Colbert Howell.

Previous page: Plan HPT740012, see page 20. Design ©William Poole Designs, Inc.

Back cover & page 4: Plan HPT740064, see page 72. Design by Donald A. Gardner
Architects, Inc. ©2001 by Donald A. Gardner Inc., photography courtesy of Donald
A. Gardner Architects, Inc.

10 9 8 7 6 5 4 3 2 1

Printed in the United States of America

Library of Congress Catalog Card Number: 2002112579

ISBN softcover: 1-931131-10-4

Contents

"LOOK TO THE PAST FOR GUIDANCE INTO THE FUTURE."

-ROBERT JACOB GOODKIN

Many of today's home designers find inspiration in America's architectural past, and use their new collections to recreate the flavor of picturesque historic neighborhoods. By incorporating some of the elements of traditional neighborhood design—homes in a mix of shapes and styles, all with spacious, welcoming porches—they bring the romantic images of the past to present-day streets. Inviting Porches presents a collection of homes that honor these elements; browse through the following pages to view more than 200 home designs, all with lots of space devoted to porches, decks and terraces.

For a full-color showcase of homes in a variety of styles, try our Design Gallery. "Prairies & Plains" features a fine assortment of Craftsman homes—charming smaller homes with matchstick detailing, stone accents and sturdy porch pillars. Country style—everything from elegant Victorian designs to carefree, relaxed farmhouses—is displayed in "Rockers & Swings." Homes in "Capes & Colonials" evoke traditional Early American designs, and the homes of "Courtyards & Porticos" are narrow-lot designs perfect for in-town living. Browse through "Sunshine & Shade" for a memorable selection of Mediterranean and Italianate designs, and finish up with "Getaways & Resorts," filled with vacation & waterfront homes with plenty of space to enjoy the outdoors. Once you've settled on the design that's right for you, turn to page 213 for information on ordering.

Sweet Retreat

WITH A BOLD DASH OF OLD CHARLESTON,
THIS SMART-SPACE HOME STEPS GENTLY INTO THE NEW CENTURY

Sweet Retreat

ABOVE: A splendid covered porch to the side of the plan recalls the warmth and charm of gentler times.

FOLLOWING PAGE: Plan HPT740001, a view from the front.

Photos by MWS Photo, Scott Moore — Builder: Michael Bates Homes

A HANDSOME TWO-STORY elevation of lap siding and stone set off standing-seam copper roofs designed to offer shelter as well as to deck out a perfect facade with plenty of curb appeal. Rugged stone accents and spring-white stucco columns and balustrades help to create a distinctive exterior that's well suited to any region. This stately and oh-so-pretty manor takes on the future with an interior design that's sophisticated, practical. Joyful rooms throughout the home flow with a deep level of comfort that may seem familiar. Surfing niches, growing space and open-air rooms that flex from formal to casual make up a red-hot design ethic that's better answered with homes just-right for everyday living.

Announced by a subdued entry porch, the open foyer leads to formal and casual areas, and boasts interior vistas that extend to the rear property. Square columns partially define the formal dining room—an elegant space with a box-bay window and a French door that opens to the wraparound porch. The heart of this home is a spacious central great room, which features a welcoming fireplace and a wall of windows with wide views of the rear property. Nearby, the breakfast bay allows access to both the rear covered porch and the wraparound porch. An efficient and well-organized kitchen provides a double sink and ample pantry, and two windows with views of the front and side properties.

All of the first-floor rooms offer views to the rear garden. To the left of the plan, a secluded master suite offers a tray ceiling, a knee-space vanity, garden tub and walk-in closet designed for two. A triple window in the master bedroom provides grand views and extends the spaciousness of the retreat. The central gallery hall ends in a private niche with a powder room—an arrangement that maintains privacy for the master wing.

Upstairs, each of two family bedrooms provides a separate vanity and private access to a shared full bath. A gallery hall leads to a guest suite with a walk-in closet, roomy bath and a stunning quadruple window, providing great views of the rear property. On the main floor, a service entrance from the garage leads to a laundry that provides additional storage.

DESIGN HPT740001

TOTAL: 2,845 square feet

FIRST FLOOR: 1,804 square feet

SECOND FLOOR: 1,041 square feet

BEDROOMS: 4

BATHROOMS: 3½

WIDTH: 59'-10" DEPTH: 71'-0"

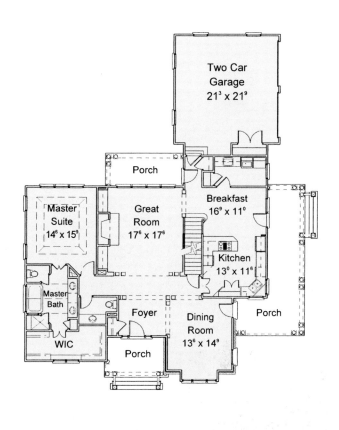

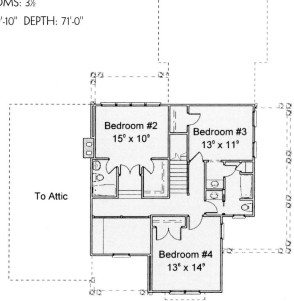

House Blend

A SAVORY COUNTRY LOOK IS A RICH BREW OF SUBTLE SOPHISTICATION, NATURAL FLAVOR AND EASY CHARM

PROMINENT TWIN GABLES and lovely bays lend just the right touch to the engaging facade of this sophisticated country home. A glass-paneled entry announces the bright foyer, which opens on each side to a formal room. French doors lead out to the front covered porch from the living and dining rooms—a perfect arrangement for entertaining. Decorative columns help define the open, two-story great room, which has a centered fireplace and access to the rear porch. A curved balcony borders a versatile loft/study, which overlooks the casual living area.

Open planning allows the warmth and beauty of the hearth to extend to the breakfast room, where family members can enjoy informal meals. The kitchen overlooks a functional ledge to a bounty of outdoor views through the breakfast area's bay window and stunning French doors, which lead to the rear porch. An ample pantry adjoins both the kitchen and the formal dining room, which is spacious enough to accommodate crowd-size events as well as quiet gatherings.

The left wing of the house is dedicated to the homeowner's retreat. A tray ceiling highlights the master bedroom, while three lovely windows and a

House Blend

French door serve to further brighten its interior. A hall with linen storage leads to one of two walk-in closets and a dressing area. The master bath features a garden tub, a separate shower and a knee-space vanity framed by separate lavatories.

A balcony hall with an overlook to the foyer wraps the stairwell and leads to the loft/study, which has a niche with built-in shelves. This sitting area is well suited to quiet study or lively conversation and is enhanced by the great room's fireplace just below. Here, the crackling of the fire in the hearth can mingle with the dusky hues of sunset and the sound of laughter from cozy family get-togethers.

One of the three second-floor bedrooms has a walk-in closet and a private bath—a perfect space for a guest or live-in relative. Two of these bedrooms share a full bath that includes a double-bowl lavatory, and both offer plenty of wardrobe space. The central upstairs hall leads to a sizable bonus room, bright with natural light from two skylights. This space, which is thoughtfully placed above the garage, is also accessible from the back staircase and may be used as a recreation room or a home office.

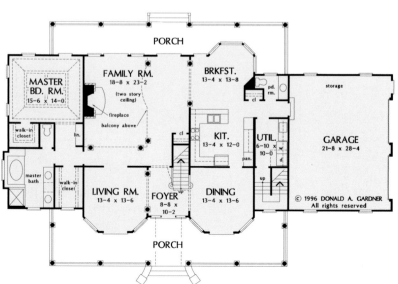

© 1996 DONALD A. GARDNER
All rights reserved

DESIGN HPT740002

TOTAL: 3,163 square feet
FIRST FLOOR: 2,086 square feet
SECOND FLOOR: 1,077 square feet
BONUS SPACE: 403 square feet
BEDROOMS: 4
BATHROOMS: 3½
WIDTH: 81'-10" DEPTH: 51'-8"

This home, as shown in the photograph, may differ from the actual blueprints.
For more detailed information, please check the floor plans carefully.

Photo by Larry E. Belk Designs

DESIGN HPT740003

TOTAL: 2,988 square feet

FIRST FLOOR: 2,096 square feet

SECOND FLOOR: 892 square feet

BEDROOMS: 3

BATHROOMS: 3½

WIDTH: 58'-0" **DEPTH:** 54'-0"

THE VARIETY IN THE ROOFLINES of this striking waterfront home will certainly make it the envy of the neighborhood. The two-story great room, with its fireplace and built-ins, is a short flight down from the foyer. The three sets of French doors give access to the covered lanai. The huge well-equipped kitchen will easily serve the gourmet who loves to entertain. The step ceiling and bay window of the dining room will add style to every meal. The master suite completes the first level. Two bedrooms and two full baths, along with an expansive loft, constitute the second level. Bedroom 3 has an attached sun deck.

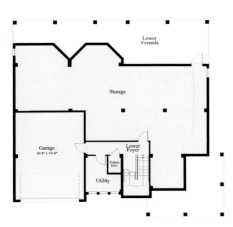

Designer showcase

DESIGN HPT740004

SQUARE FOOTAGE: 3,098

BONUS SPACE: 849 square feet

BEDROOMS: 3

BATHROOMS: 4

WIDTH: 78'-0" DEPTH: 75'-4"

DENTILS ACCENT THE HIPPED ROOF, while white double columns outline the entry of this lovely three-bedroom home. Formal entertaining sits up front in the entry design. Tucked out of sight from the living room yet close to the dining area, the island kitchen features acres of counter space and a convenient utility room. The breakfast nook sits open to the family room, sharing the spacious views and warming fireplace of this open and relaxing informal zone. A wonderful master suite fills the right side of the plan with luxury elements, such as a sitting room, large walk-in closet and soaking tub. Two family bedrooms to the left of the plan share a full bath.

REAR VIEW

This home, as shown in the photograph, may differ from the actual blueprints.
For more detailed information, please check the floor plans carefully.

Photo by Living Home Concepts Home Planning

HERE'S AN UPSCALE multi-level

plan with expansive rear views. The first floor provides an open living and dining area, defined by decorative columns and enhanced by natural light from tall windows. A breakfast area with a lovely triple window opens to a sun room, which allows light to pour into the gourmet kitchen. The master wing features a tray ceiling in the bedroom, two walk-in closets and an elegant private vestibule leading to a lavish bath. Upstairs, a reading loft overlooks the great room and leads to a sleeping area with two suites.

DESIGN HPT740005

TOTAL: 3,313 square feet

FIRST FLOOR: 2,391 square feet

SECOND FLOOR: 922 square feet

FINISHED BASEMENT: 1,964 square feet

BONUS SPACE: 400 square feet

BEDROOMS: 3

BATHROOMS: 3½

WIDTH: 63'-10" DEPTH: 85'-6"

Photo by Raef Gohne Photography

This home, as shown in the photograph, may differ from the actual blueprints. For more detailed information, please check the floor plans carefully.

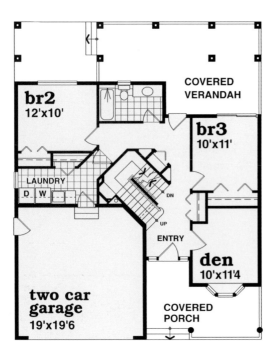

DESIGN HPT740006

TOTAL: 2,163 square feet

FIRST FLOOR: 832 square feet

SECOND FLOOR: 1,331 square feet

BEDROOMS: 3

BATHROOMS: 2½

WIDTH: 37'-6" DEPTH: 48'-4"

THIS HOME OFFERS TWO STORIES, with a twist! The living spaces are on the second floor and include a living/dining room combination with a deck and fireplace. The family room also has a fireplace, plus a built-in entertainment center, and is open to the skylit kitchen. The master bedroom is also on this level and features a private bath. Downtstairs, family bedrooms, a full bath and a cozy den reside on the first level.

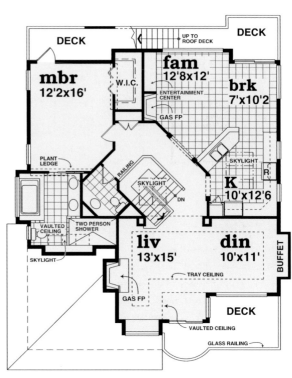

This home, as shown in the photograph, may differ from the actual blueprints.
For more detailed information, please check the floor plans carefully.

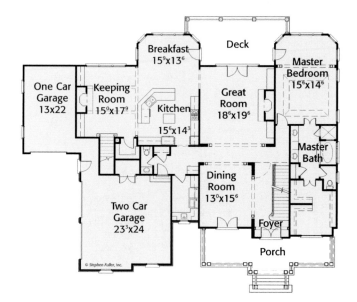

DESIGN HPT740007

TOTAL: 4,403 square feet

FIRST FLOOR: 2,628 square feet

SECOND FLOOR: 1,775 square feet

BEDROOMS: 5

BATHROOMS: 3½

WIDTH: 79'-6" DEPTH: 65'-1"

WITH FIVE BEDROOMS and a wonderful stone-and-siding exterior, this country home will satisfy every need. Two sets of French doors provide access to the dining room and foyer. The great room enjoys a warming fireplace and deck access. The kitchen, breakfast bay and keeping room feature an open floor plan. A charming sitting area in a bay window sets off the master bedroom. The master bath features a large walk-in closet, two-sink vanity, separate tub and shower and compartmented toilet. Four bedrooms, an office and two full baths complete the upper level. This home is designed with a walkout basement foundation.

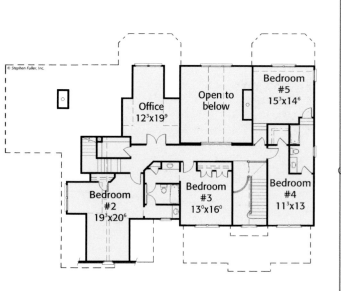

Designer showcase

This home, as shown in the photograph, may differ from the actual blueprints. For more detailed information, please check the floor plans carefully.

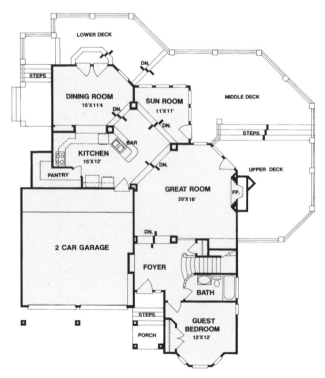

LOWER DECK

STEPS

DINING ROOM
15'X11'4

SUN ROOM
11'X11'

MIDDLE DECK

DN.

KITCHEN
15'X12'

BAR

PANTRY

DN.

UPPER DECK

GREAT ROOM
20'X18'

FP.

2 CAR GARAGE

DN.

FOYER

BATH

STEPS

PORCH

GUEST
BEDROOM
12'X12'

DESIGN HPT740008

TOTAL: 2,652 square feet

FIRST FLOOR: 1,309 square feet

SECOND FLOOR: 1,343 square feet

BEDROOMS: 3

BATHROOMS: 3

WIDTH: 44'-4" DEPTH: 58'-2"

L

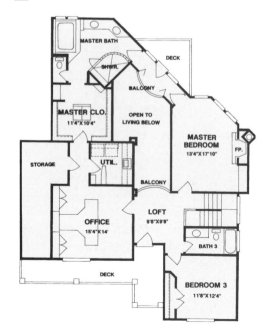

MASTER BATH

SHWR.

DECK

BALCONY

MASTER CLO.
11'4"X10'4"

OPEN TO
LIVING BELOW

MASTER
BEDROOM
13'4"X17'10"

FP.

STORAGE

UTIL.

BALCONY

OFFICE
15'4"X14'

LOFT
9'8"X9'8"

BATH 3

DECK

BEDROOM 3
11'8"X12'4"

CLEAN, CONTEMPORARY LINES, a unique floor plan and a metal roof with a cupola set this farmhouse apart. Remote-control transoms in the cupola open to create an airy and decidedly unique foyer. The great room, sun room, dining room and kitchen flow from one to another for casual entertaining with flair. The rear of the home is fashioned with plenty of windows overlooking the multi-level deck. A front bedroom and bath would make a comfortable guest suite. The master bedroom and bath upstairs are bridged by a pipe-rail balcony that also gives access to a rear deck. An additional bedroom, home office and bath complete this very special plan.

This home, as shown in the photograph, may differ from the actual blueprints. For more detailed information, please check the floor plans carefully.

Photo courtesy of Chatham Home Planning Inc., Chris A. Little of Atlanta Photographer

Master Bedroom 16'6"x 19'

Bedroom 13'x 13'

Balcony

DESIGN HPT740009

TOTAL: 1,863 square feet

FIRST FLOOR: 1,056 square feet

SECOND FLOOR: 807 square feet

BEDROOMS: 4

BATHROOMS: 3

WIDTH: 33'-0" DEPTH: 54'-0"

RUN UP A FLIGHT OF STAIRS to an attractive four-bedroom home! With a traditional flavor, this fine pier design is sure to please. The living room features a fireplace and easy access to the L-shaped kitchen. Here, a work island makes meal preparation a breeze. Two family bedrooms share a full bath and access to the laundry facilities. Upstairs, the master bedroom provides a master bath and His and Hers closets, while a third bedroom offers a private bath and two walk-in closets. Please specify crawlspace or pier foundation when ordering.

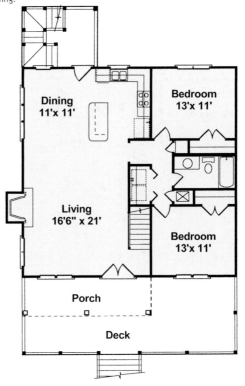

Dining 11'x 11'

Bedroom 13'x 11'

Living 16'6" x 21'

Bedroom 13'x 11'

Porch

Deck

Designer showcase

This home, as shown in the photograph, may differ from the actual blueprints.
For more detailed information, please check the floor plans carefully.

DESIGN HPT740010

SQUARE FOOTAGE: 1,832

BONUS SPACE: 425 square feet

BEDROOMS: 3

BATHROOMS: 2

WIDTH: 65'-4"   DEPTH: 62'-0"

THIS CHARMING COUNTRY PLAN boasts a cathedral ceiling in the great room. Dormer windows shed light on the foyer, which opens to a front bedroom/study and to the formal dining room. The kitchen is completely open to the great room and features a stylish snack-bar island and a bay window in the breakfast nook. The master suite offers a tray ceiling and a skylit bath. Two secondary bedrooms share a full bath on the opposite side of the house. Bonus space over the garage may be developed in the future.

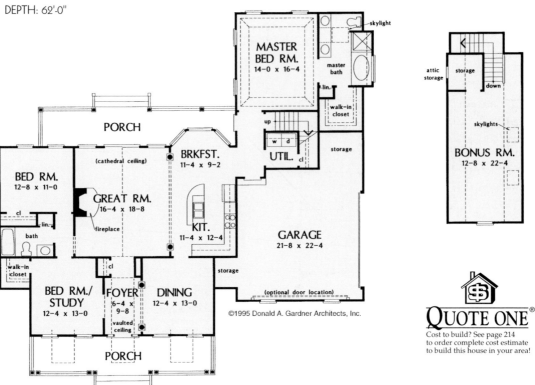

©1995 Donald A. Gardner Architects, Inc.

QUOTE ONE®

Cost to build? See page 214
to order complete cost estimate
to build this house in your area!

This home, as shown in the photograph, may differ from the actual blueprints.
For more detailed information, please check the floor plans carefully.

THIS THREE-BEDROOM HOME entices with a gratifying exterior and a livable floor plan. Bedrooms 2 and 3 are divided by a full hall bath on the right side of the home. The master bedroom features a full master bath with a walk-in closet, dual vanities, a whirlpool tub and separate shower. A warming fireplace and built-in shelves accent the family room. Adjacent to the dining room, the kitchen holds a walk-in pantry and a bayed breakfast area. The roomy utility room is spacious and serves as a pass-through to the garage.

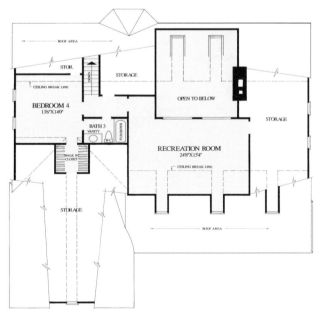

DESIGN HPT740011

SQUARE FOOTAGE: 2,151 square feet

BONUS SPACE: 814 square feet

BEDROOMS: 3

BATHROOMS: 2

WIDTH: 61'-0" **DEPTH:** 59'-0"

Designer showcase

This home, as shown in the photograph, may differ from the actual blueprints.
For more detailed information, please check the floor plans carefully.

DESIGN HPT740012

TOTAL: 4,246 square feet

FIRST FLOOR: 2,986 square feet

SECOND FLOOR: 1,260 square feet

BONUS SPACE: 758 square feet

BEDROOMS: 4

BATHROOMS: 4½ +½

WIDTH: 105'-0" DEPTH: 69'-0"

APPEALING BOTH INSIDE AND OUT, this plan suits a family's every need. Inside, the foyer opens to the dining room and the living room/library which features a fireplace. The island kitchen includes a breakfast area and leads to the laundry room and garage. To the right of the family room is the powder room and the master bedroom with an exclusive master bath. Upstairs, each of the three family bedrooms contains a private full baths and a walk-in closet. A future recreation room and an additional bedroom are available to the far left of this design.

This home, as shown in the photograph, may differ from the actual blueprints. For more detailed information, please check the floor plans carefully.

DESIGN HPT740013

TOTAL: 3,201 square feet

FIRST FLOOR: 2,200 square feet

SECOND FLOOR: 1,001 square feet

BONUS SPACE: 694 square feet

BEDROOMS: 4

BATHROOMS: 3½

WIDTH: 70'-4" **DEPTH:** 74'-4"

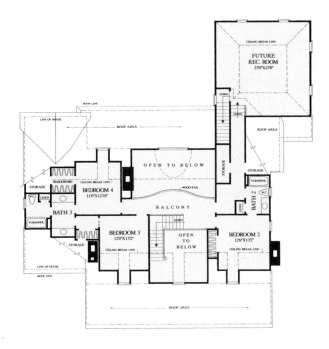

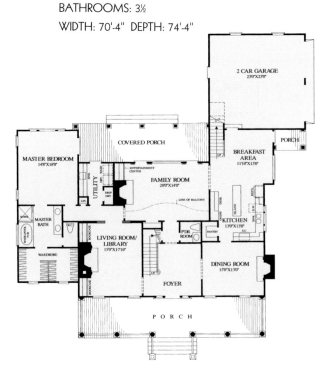

THIS WELL-THOUGHT-OUT PLAN allows for household members to plan separate events in one evening. The family room and the living room/library, both feature a fireplaces and built-ins. The pass-through kitchen includes an island and connects the breakfast area and dining room. Accessible to the covered porch, the master bedroom provides a full private bath and His and Her closets. On the second floor are three additional bedrooms and a balcony overlooking the first-floor family room. The two-car garage protects vehicles from unpleasant weather.

Designer showcase

21

Photo courtesy of Breland & Farmer Designers, Inc.

This home, as shown in the photograph, may differ from the actual blueprints. For more detailed information, please check the floor plans carefully.

DESIGN HPT740014

TOTAL: 3,119 square feet

FIRST FLOOR: 2,092 square feet

SECOND FLOOR: 1,027 square feet

BEDROOMS: 4

BATHROOMS: 3½

WIDTH: 66'-0" DEPTH: 80'-0"

THIS SOUTHERN PLANTATION HOME, featuring traditional accents such as front-facing dormers, a covered front porch and a stucco-and-brick facade, will be the delight of any fine neighborhood. Inside, a study and formal dining room flank the foyer. The family room shares a two-sided fireplace with the refreshing sun room, which overlooks the rear deck. The kitchen shares space with an eating area overlooking the front yard. The first-floor master suite features a large closet and a private bath. Three additional bedrooms and two baths are located upstairs.

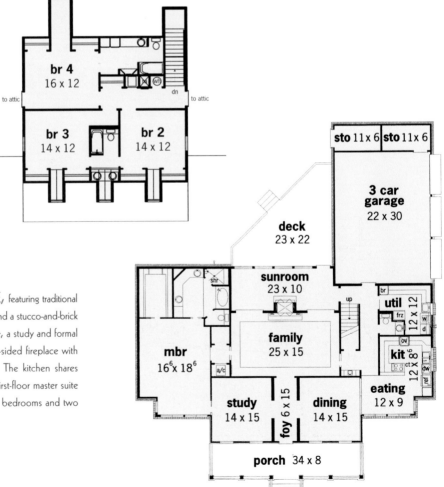

DESIGN HPT740015

SQUARE FOOTAGE: 1,864

BONUS SPACE: 420 square feet

BEDROOMS: 3

BATHROOMS: 2½

WIDTH: 70'-4" **DEPTH:** 56'-4"

QUAINT AND COZY ON THE OUTSIDE WITH PORCHES front and back, this three-bedroom country home surprises with an open floor plan featuring a large great room with a cathedral ceiling. A central kitchen with an angled counter opens to the breakfast and great rooms for easy entertaining. The privately located master bedroom has a cathedral ceiling and access to the deck. Two secondary bedrooms share a full hall bath. A bonus room makes expanding easy.

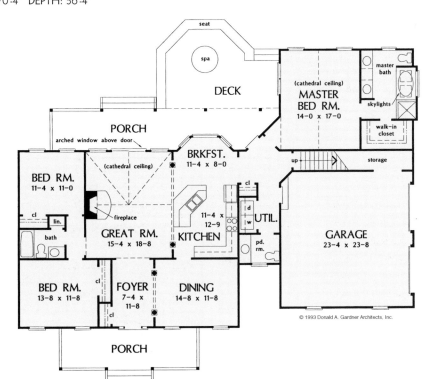

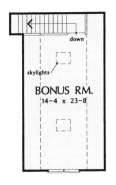

© 1993 Donald A. Gardner Architects, Inc.

Quote One®

Cost to build? See page 214
to order complete cost estimate
to build this house in your area!

Designer showcase

This home, as shown in the photograph, may differ from the actual blueprints. For more detailed information, please check the floor plans carefully.

DESIGN HPT740016

TOTAL: 2,457 square feet

FIRST FLOOR: 1,819 square feet

SECOND FLOOR: 638 square feet

BONUS SPACE: 385 square feet

BEDROOMS: 3

BATHROOMS: 2½

WIDTH: 47'-4"   DEPTH: 82'-8"

WITH THE CAPABILITY of residing on a narrow lot, this home fits just as nicely in wide open spaces. Inside, the master bedroom provides homeowners with a private mster bath and a view to the front yard. The island kitchen is near the dinning room, includes a breakfast area and a snack bar. The family room is spacious, it contains a hearth and built-ins. Two family bedrooms and a full hall bath are available on the second floor

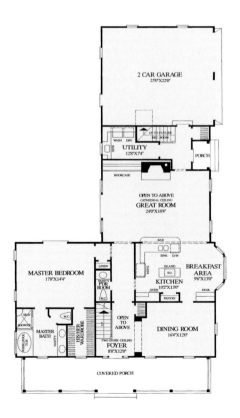

This home, as shown in the photograph, may differ from the actual blueprints.
For more detailed information, please check the floor plans carefully.

Photo courtesy of Stephen Fuller, Inc.

A SYMMETRICAL FACADE with twin chimneys makes a grand statement on this home. A covered porch welcomes visitors and provides a pleasant place to spend a mild evening. The entry foyer is flanked by formal living areas—a dining room and a living room—each with a fireplace. A third fireplace is the highlight of the expansive great room to the rear. An L-shaped kitchen offers a work island and a walk-in pantry as amenities and easily serves the nearby breakfast and sun rooms. The master suite provides lavish luxuries. This home is designed with a walkout basement foundation.

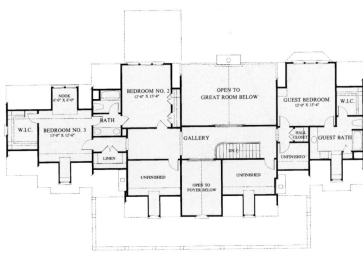

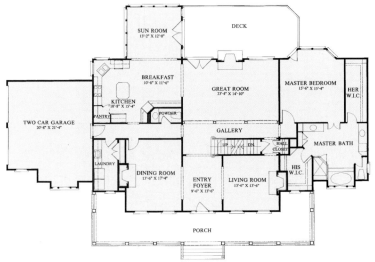

DESIGN HPT740017

TOTAL: 3,940 square feet

FIRST FLOOR: 2,565 square feet

SECOND FLOOR: 1,375 square feet

BEDROOMS: 4

BATHROOMS: 3½

WIDTH: 88'-6" DEPTH: 58'-6"

Cost to build? See page 214
to order complete cost estimate
to build this house in your area!

Designer showcase

Photo courtesy of Stephen Fuller, Inc.

This home, as shown in the photograph, may differ from the actual blueprints. For more detailed information, please check the floor plans carefully.

DESIGN HPT740018

TOTAL: 3,675 square feet
FIRST FLOOR: 2,380 square feet
SECOND FLOOR: 1,295 square feet
BEDROOMS: 4
BATHROOMS: 3½
WIDTH: 77'-4" DEPTH: 58'-4"

FINELY CRAFTED PORCHES—front, side and rear—make this home a classic in traditional Southern living. Past the large French doors, the impressive foyer is flanked by the formal living and dining rooms. Beyond the stair is a vaulted great room with an expanse of windows, a fireplace and built-in bookcases. From here, the breakfast room and kitchen are easily accessible and open to a private side porch. The master suite provides a large bath, two spacious closets, a fireplace and a private entry that opens to the covered rear porch. The second floor contains three bedrooms—each with private access to a bath—and a playroom. This home is designed with a walkout basement foundation.

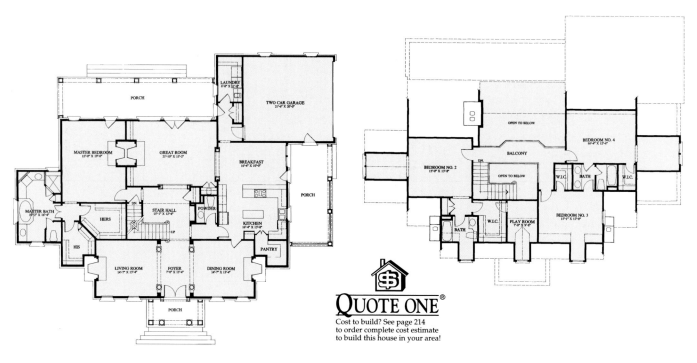

QUOTE ONE®

Cost to build? See page 214
to order complete cost estimate
to build this house in your area!

This home, as shown in the photograph, may differ from the actual blueprints.
For more detailed information, please check the floor plans carefully.

Photo by Mark Englund

DESIGN HPT740019

SQUARE FOOTAGE: 1,655
BEDROOMS: 3
BATHROOMS: 2
WIDTH: 52'-0" DEPTH: 66'-0"

ELEGANTLY ARCHED doors and windows decorate the exterior of this fine home, which offers an intriguing floor plan. The living room features a soaring fifteen-foot ceiling and adjoins the octagonal dining room. Both rooms offer views of the skylit rear porch; a skylight also brightens the kitchen. The lavish master suite includes a walk-in closet, access to a small side porch and a full bath with a corner marble tub. Two additional bedrooms, thoughtfully placed apart from the master suite, share a full bath. Please specify crawlspace or slab foundation when ordering.

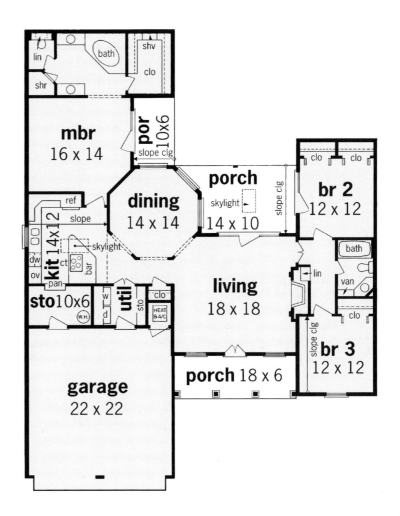

Designer showcase

DESIGN HPT740020

SQUARE FOOTAGE: 1,787

BONUS SPACE: 326 square feet

BEDROOMS: 3

BATHROOMS: 2

WIDTH: 66'-2" DEPTH: 66'-8"

A NEIGHBORLY PORCH as friendly as a handshake wraps around this charming country home. Inside, cathedral ceilings promote a feeling of spaciousness. The great room is enhanced with a fireplace and built-in bookshelves. A uniquely shaped formal dining room separates the kitchen and breakfast area. Outdoor pursuits—rain or shine—will be enjoyed from the screened porch. The master suite is located at the rear of the plan for privacy and features a walk-in closet and a luxurious bath. Two additional bedrooms— one with a walk-in closet—share a skylit bath.

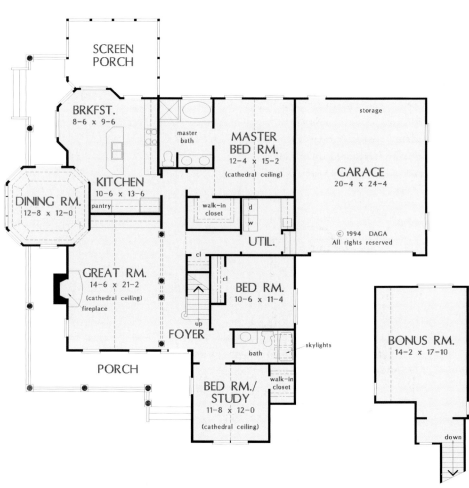

This home, as shown in the photograph, may differ from the actual blueprints.
For more detailed information, please check the floor plans carefully.

THE FARMHOUSE APPEAL of this four-bedroom home is in the wraparound, covered porch—perfect for rocking away the afternoons. The exterior detailing adds the look of yesteryear, but the inside floor plan brings things up-to-date. You can easily unload a station wagon full of groceries using the quick path from garage to kitchen and then warm up by the see-through fireplace. The spacious great room is enhanced by a bay window and shares the through-fireplace with the kitchen. Upstairs, four bedrooms include a pampering master suite. The master bath includes His and Hers sinks, a tub, separate shower and spacious walk-in closet.

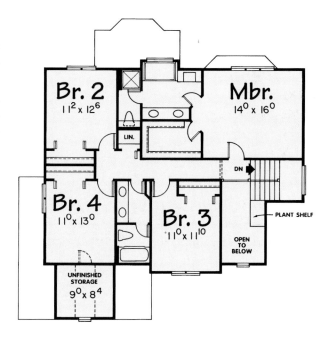

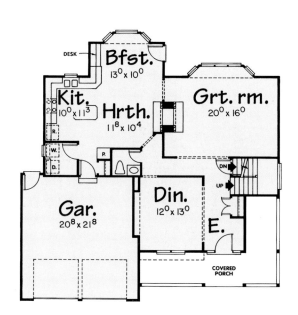

DESIGN HPT740021

TOTAL: 2,292 square feet

FIRST FLOOR: 1,158 square feet

SECOND FLOOR: 1,134 square feet

BEDROOMS: 4

BATHROOMS: 2½

WIDTH: 46'-0" DEPTH: 47'-10"

Designer showcase

Photo courtesy of Stephen Fuller, Inc.

This home, as shown in the photograph, may differ from the actual blueprints. For more detailed information, please check the floor plans carefully.

DESIGN HPT740022

TOTAL: 3,186 square feet

FIRST FLOOR: 2,081 square feet

SECOND FLOOR: 1,105 square feet

BEDROOMS: 4

BATHROOMS: 3½

WIDTH: 69'-9"   DEPTH: 65'-0"

QUOTE ONE®

Cost to build? See page 214
to order complete cost estimate
to build this house in your area!

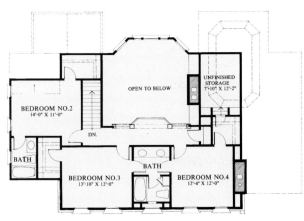

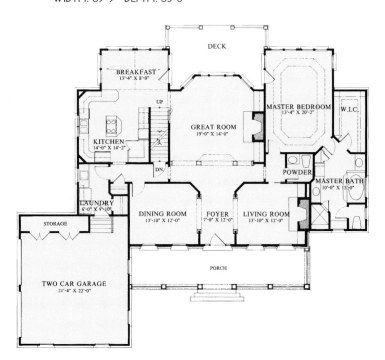

FROM ITS PEDIMENT to the columned porch, this Georgian facade is impressive. Inside, classical symmetry balances the living and dining rooms on either side of the foyer. The two-story great room features built-in cabinetry, a fireplace and a large bay window. The island kitchen opens to the breakfast area. The master suite boasts a tray ceiling, a wall of glass and access to the rear deck, as well as a private bath. Three second-floor family bedrooms boast walk-in closets. This home is designed with a walkout basement foundation.

This home, as shown in the photograph, may differ from the actual blueprints.
For more detailed information, please check the floor plans carefully.

DESIGN HPT740023

TOTAL: 2,069 square feet

FIRST FLOOR: 1,075 square feet

SECOND FLOOR: 994 square feet

BONUS SPACE: 382 square feet

BEDROOMS: 3

BATHROOMS: 2½

WIDTH: 56'-4" DEPTH: 35'-4"

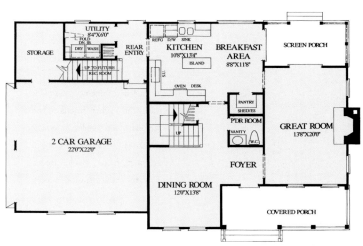

To LIVE IN THIS ADORABLE two-story home will be like living a childhood dream. The happy facade features windows accented by shutters and a covered porch with ornamental railing. Open living areas create an abundance of space on the first floor—an island kitchen, breakfast area, dining room and family room with a hearth and access to the rear porch. Near the rear entry is the utility room and the garage with extra storage space. Sleeping quarters can be found upstairs with two family bedrooms and a master bedroom. The master bedroom includes a private bath with a walk-in closet, whirlpool tub and separate shower.

Designer showcase

This home, as shown in the photograph, may differ from the actual blueprints. For more detailed information, please check the floor plans carefully.

DESIGN HPT740024

TOTAL: 2,631 square feet

FIRST FLOOR: 1,273 square feet

SECOND FLOOR: 1,358 square feet

BEDROOMS: 4

BATHROOMS: 3½

WIDTH: 54'-10" DEPTH: 48'-6"

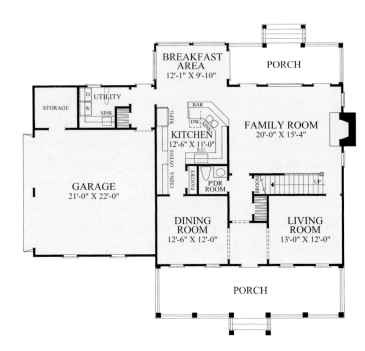

THIS TWO-STORY HOME SUITS the needs of each household member. Family gatherings are not crowded with a spacious family room, which is adjacent to the kitchen and the breakfast area. Just beyond the foyer, the dining and living rooms have a view to the front yard. The master bedroom features its own full bath with dual-vanities, whirlpool tub and separate shower. Three family bedrooms are available upstairs—one with a walk-in closet—and two full hall baths. Extra storage space is found in the two car garage.

DESIGN HPT740025

TOTAL: 2,135 square feet

FIRST FLOOR: 1,050 square feet

SECOND FLOOR: 1,085 square feet

BEDROOMS: 4

BATHROOMS: 2½

WIDTH: 50'-8" DEPTH: 39'-4"

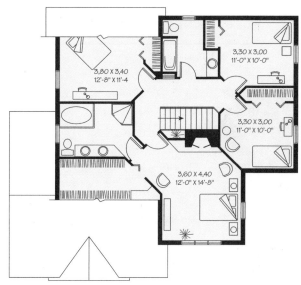

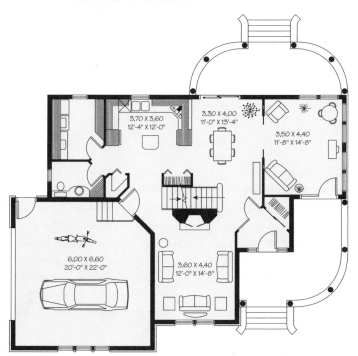

THIS LOVELY COUNTRY DESIGN features a stunning wrapping porch and plenty of windows to provide the interior with natural light. The living room boasts a centered fireplace, which helps to define this spacious open area. A nine-foot ceiling on the first floor adds a sense of spaciousness and light. The casual living room leads outdoors to a rear porch. Upstairs, four bedrooms cluster around a central hall. The master suite sports a walk-in closet and a deluxe bath with an oval tub and a separate shower. This home is designed with a basement foundation.

Homes for wide open spaces

DESIGN HPT740026

TOTAL: 1,811 square feet

FIRST FLOOR: 916 square feet

SECOND FLOOR: 895 square feet

BONUS SPACE: 262 square feet

BEDROOMS: 3

BATHROOMS: 2½

WIDTH: 44'-0" DEPTH: 38'-0"

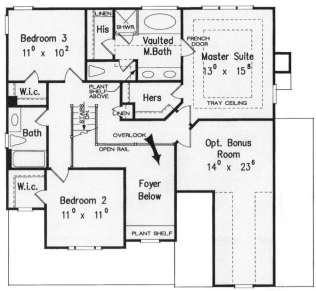

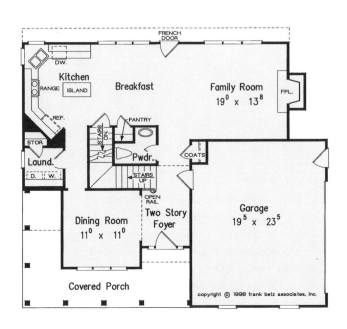

GABLES AT VARYING HEIGHTS, a traditional front porch and shuttered windows give a small-town look to this family home. The two-story foyer leads to the dining room on the left or to the family room, which is straight ahead past the powder room, coat closet and entrance to the garage. The family room is open to the kitchen, which boasts a work island, corner window sink and access to the laundry room. The second floor provides a master suite that contains two walk-in closets, two family bedrooms that share a bath but have private walk-in closets, an overlook to the foyer below and an optional bonus room. Please specify basement or crawlspace foundation when ordering.

DESIGN HPT740027

TOTAL: 2,034 square feet

FIRST FLOOR: 1,559 square feet

SECOND FLOOR: 475 square feet

BONUS SPACE: 321 square feet

BEDROOMS: 4

BATHROOMS: 3

WIDTH: 50'-0" **DEPTH:** 56'-4"

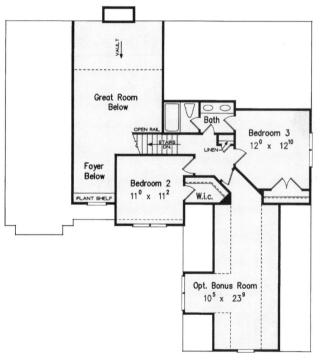

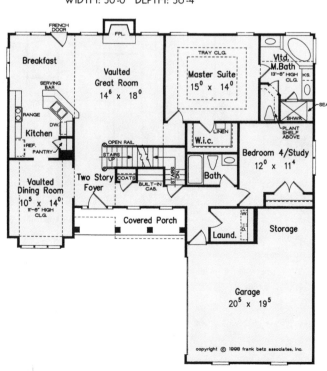

A CAREFUL BLEND OF SIDING AND STONE lends eye-catching appeal to this traditional plan. Vaulted ceilings grace the great room, master bath and dining room. The efficient kitchen offers pantry storage and a serving bar to the breakfast room. The master suite features a tray ceiling and a deluxe private bath. A bedroom/study is located on the first floor. Two second-floor bedrooms easily access a full bath. An optional bonus room offers plenty of room to grow—making it perfect for a guest suite, home office or exercise room. Please specify basement or crawlspace foundation when ordering.

Homes for wide open spaces

DESIGN HPT740028

TOTAL: 2,451 square feet

FIRST FLOOR: 1,797 square feet

SECOND FLOOR: 654 square feet

BONUS SPACE: 266 square feet

BEDROOMS: 3

BATHROOMS: 2½

WIDTH: 54'-0" DEPTH: 54'-10"

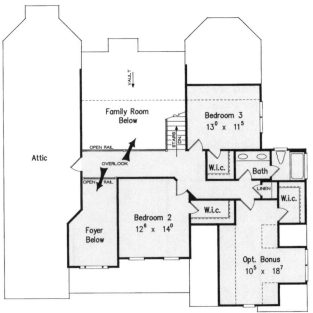

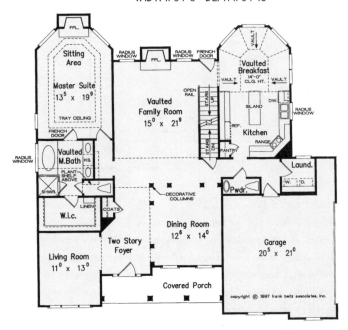

CAPSTONES AND BRICK ACCENTS add a touch of class to the charm and comfort of this American dream home. A vaulted breakfast bay brings the outdoors in and fills a sophisticated gourmet kitchen with natural light. The spacious family room enjoys radius windows and a French door to the back property, while a private formal living room opens off the foyer. A centered fireplace flanked by windows dresses up the master suite, which also features a vaulted private bath with a whirlpool tub. The second-floor bedrooms are connected by a balcony hall with overlooks the family room and the foyer. Please specify basement or crawlspace foundation when ordering.

DESIGN HPT740029

TOTAL: 1,492 square feet

FIRST FLOOR: 757 square feet

SECOND FLOOR: 735 square feet

BEDROOMS: 3

BATHROOMS: 2½

WIDTH: 47'-0" DEPTH: 42'-0"

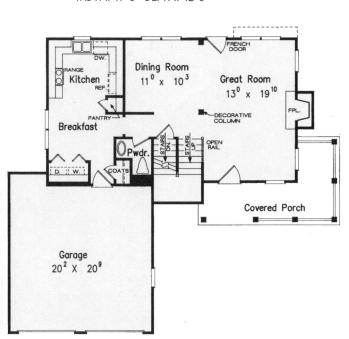

A WRAPAROUND PORCH FEATURING Victorian accents and a multitude of other delightful details combine to give this home plenty of curb appeal. The entry announces the great room and dining area, defined by decorative columns. A U-shaped kitchen serves both the breakfast area and the dining room. The great room offers a fireplace as an accent and opens to the rear property through a French door. Upstairs, the master suite provides a vaulted ceiling, garden tub with radius window and walk-in closet. Each of the two additional bedrooms offers a wide wardrobe. Please specify basement, crawlspace or slab foundation when ordering.

Homes for wide open spaces

DESIGN HPT740030

TOTAL: 2,089 square feet

FIRST FLOOR: 1,146 square feet

SECOND FLOOR: 943 square feet

BONUS SPACE: 324 square feet

BEDROOMS: 3

BATHROOMS: 2½

WIDTH: 56'-0" **DEPTH:** 38'-0"

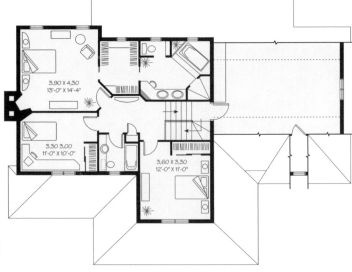

THIS BEAUTIFUL THREE-BEDROOM HOME boasts many attractive features. Two covered porches will entice you outside, while inside, a special sun room on the first floor brings the outdoors in. The foyer opens on the right to a comfortable family room that may be used as a home office. On the left, the living area is warmed by the sun room and a cozy corner fireplace. A formal dining area lies adjacent to an efficient kitchen with a central island and breakfast nook overlooking the back porch. The second level offers two family bedrooms served by a full bath. A spacious master suite with a walk-in closet and luxurious bath completes the second floor. This home is designed with a daylight basement.

DESIGN HPT740031

TOTAL: 4,211 square feet

FIRST FLOOR: 2,113 square feet

SECOND FLOOR: 2,098 square feet

BEDROOMS: 5

BATHROOMS: 4½

WIDTH: 68'-6" DEPTH: 53'-0"

WITH A WRAPAROUND PORCH, eyebrow dormer, gables and shutters, this amazing farmhouse is as charming on the outside as it is inside. Enter the foyer, formal dining and living areas and the gallery hallway from the front porch. A circular stair presents a wonderful first impression in the two-story foyer. Note the triangular island and octagonal breakfast area in the large gourmet kitchen. A beautiful fireplace with built-in shelving adorns the two-story family room. The second floor includes three family bedrooms and a luxurious master suite. Please specify basement, crawlspace or slab foundation when ordering.

DESIGN HPT740032

TOTAL: 2,262 square feet

FIRST FLOOR: 1,784 square feet

SECOND FLOOR: 478 square feet

BONUS SPACE: 336 square feet

BEDROOMS: 3

BATHROOMS: 2½

WIDTH: 54'-0" DEPTH: 54'-6"

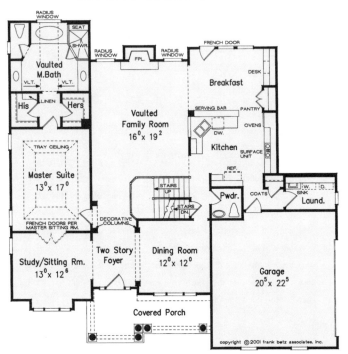

THIS FARMHOUSE-STYLE, three-bedroom home holds a spacious floor plan. The vaulted family room joins the breakfast room and kitchen for everyday affairs, but is near a formal dining room for more special occasions. The master suite on the first floor opens to a sitting room or study. The master bath ensures a wonderful retreat with its two walk-in closets, two vanities and a compartmented toilet area. Two family bedrooms on the second floor are joined by bonus space of 336 square feet that can be developed later. Please specify basement or crawlspace foundation when ordering.

40

DESIGN HPT740033

TOTAL: 3,843 square feet

FIRST FLOOR: 1,992 square feet

SECOND FLOOR: 1,851 square feet

BEDROOMS: 5

BATHROOMS: 4½

WIDTH: 66'-4"   DEPTH: 53'-0"

THIS SOUTHERN HOME has a strong classic nature that's enhanced by the asymmetrical patterns created by the hipped roofline and window placement. A spacious, open floor plan greets you upon entering, with an array of columns defining the formal dining room and living room. The focal point of the two-story entry is the sweeping circular staircase that rises to a balcony overlooking both the foyer and the great room. The breakfast nook is situated between the island kitchen and the great room, where a wall of windows looks out to the rear property. Bedroom 5 is found tucked away on the left, creating privacy for overnight guests. The immensely lavish master suite resides on the second floor, where a sitting room offers a quiet retreat. Please specify basement or crawl-space foundation when ordering.

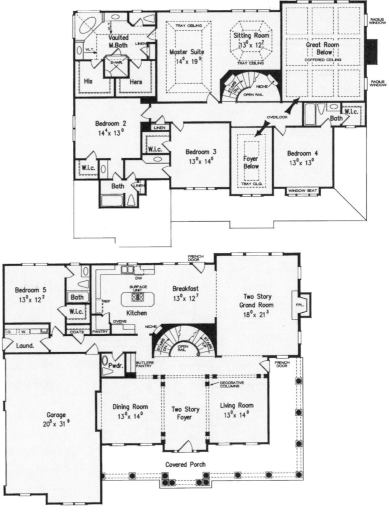

DESIGN HPT740034

TOTAL: 2,884 square feet

FIRST FLOOR: 2,247 square feet

SECOND FLOOR: 637 square feet

BONUS SPACE: 235 square feet

BEDROOMS: 4

BATHROOMS: 4

WIDTH: 64'-0" DEPTH: 55'-2"

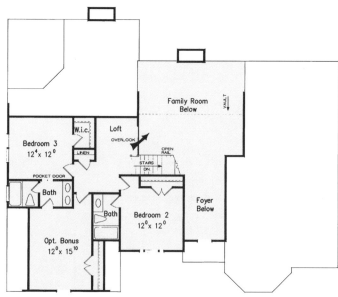

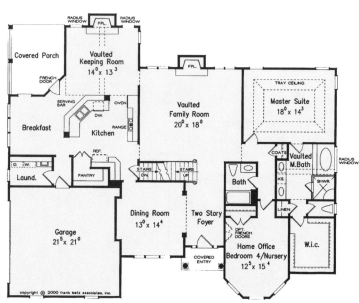

THIS ASTONISHING TRADITIONAL HOME looks great with its gables, muntin windows, keystone lintels and turret-style bay. Inside, the heart of the home is the vaulted family room with a fireplace. The kitchen conveniently connects to the dining room, breakfast room and garage. The master bath leads into a walk-in closet. The home office or nursery near the hall bath is illuminated by a bayed wall of windows and could become an additional family bedroom. Family bedrooms upstairs share a loft that overlooks the family room. Please specify basement or crawlspace foundation when ordering.

DESIGN HPT740035

TOTAL: 3,285 square feet

FIRST FLOOR: 2,293 square feet

SECOND FLOOR: 992 square feet

BONUS SPACE: 131 square feet

BEDROOMS: 4

BATHROOMS: 3½

WIDTH: 71'-0" DEPTH: 62'-0"

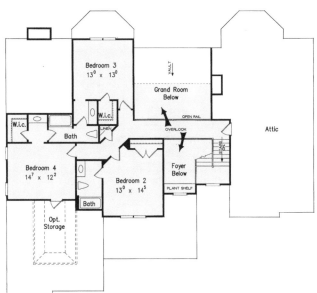

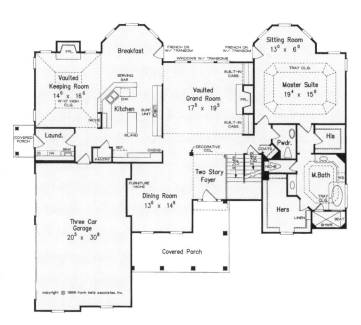

A COMBINATION OF STONE, siding and multiple rooflines creates a cottage feel to this large home. Inside, the grand room and keeping room both feature fireplaces and vaulted ceilings—the grand room features built-in cabinets, a fireplace, and windows with transoms. A sumptuous master suite enjoys a sitting room, a tray ceiling, and a lavish private bath featuring a shower with a built-in seat. The gourmet kitchen enjoys an island countertop, a serving bar, and a walk-in pantry that accesses the three-car garage. Three additional bedrooms are found upstairs with two full baths—Bedrooms 3 and 4 each include a large walk-in closet. Please specify basement or crawlspace foundation when ordering.

Homes for wide open spaces

DESIGN HPT740036

SQUARE FOOTAGE: 2,282

BONUS SPACE: 629 square feet

BEDROOMS: 3

BATHROOMS: 2

WIDTH: 60'-0" DEPTH: 75'-4"

COLUMNS AND KEYSTONE LINTELS lend a European aura to this stone-and-siding home. Arched openings and decorative columns define the formal dining room to the left of the foyer. A ribbon of windows with transoms above draws sunshine into the living room. The master suite opens from a short hallway, and enjoys a tray ceiling, vaulted bathroom with shelving, compartmented toilet, separate shower and garden tub. Transoms abound in the open informal living areas of this home. A bay windowed breakfast nook adjoins the kitchen with a central serving bar and the family room with a warming fireplace. Two additional bedrooms share a full bath to the left of the plan. Please specify basement or crawlspace foundation when ordering.

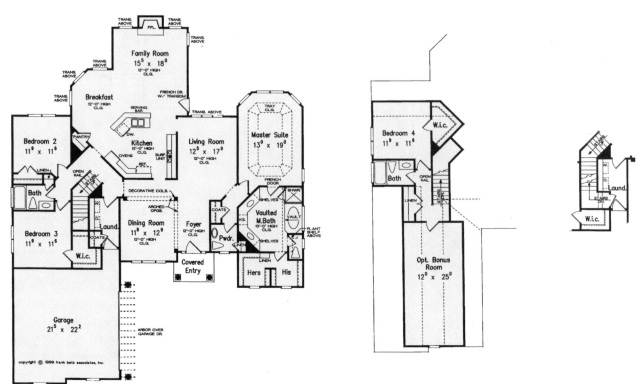

DESIGN HPT740037

SQUARE FOOTAGE: 4,038

BEDROOMS: 4

BATHROOMS: 4½

WIDTH: 98'-0" DEPTH: 90'-0"

REMINISCENT OF THE old Newport mansions, this luxury house has volume ceilings, a glamorous master suite with a hearth-warmed sitting area, a glassed-in sun room, a home office, three porches with a deck, and a gourmet kitchen with a pantry. Graceful French doors are used for all the entrances and in the formal living and dining rooms. The kitchen is magnificent and boasts a large pantry. A centrally positioned family room is graced with a large fireplace and is accessed by the rear porch, living room and dining room.

Homes for wide open spaces

DESIGN HPT740038

TOTAL: 1,939 square feet

FIRST FLOOR: 1,341 square feet

SECOND FLOOR: 598 square feet

BEDROOMS: 3

BATHROOMS: 2

WIDTH: 50'-3"   DEPTH: 46'-3"

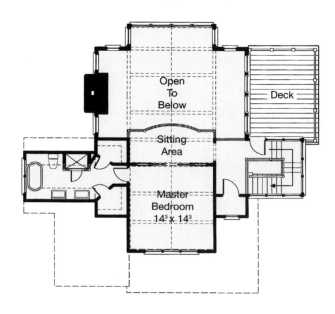

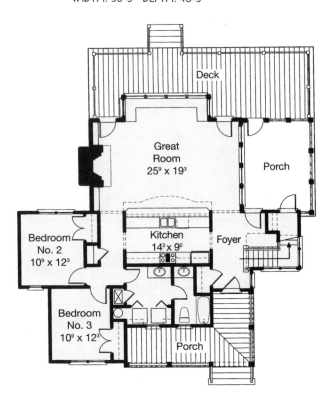

HORIZONTAL SIDING, plentiful windows and a wraparound porch grace this comfortable home. The great room is aptly named, with a fireplace, built-in seating and access to the rear deck. Meal preparation is a breeze with a galley kitchen designed for efficiency. A screened porch is available for sipping lemonade on warm summer afternoons. The first floor contains two bedrooms and a unique bath to serve family and guests. The second floor offers a private getaway with a master suite that supplies panoramic views from its adjoining sitting area. A master bath with His and Hers walk-in closets and a private deck completes the second floor.

DESIGN HPT740039

SQUARE FOOTAGE: 2,019

LOFT: 384 square feet

BEDROOMS: 3

BATHROOMS: 2

WIDTH: 56'-0" DEPTH: 56'-3"

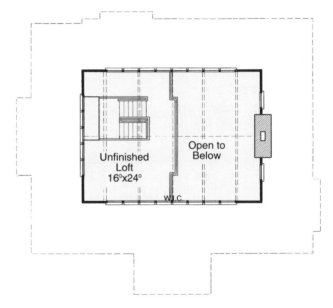

Unfinished Loft 16⁰x24⁰

Open to Below

W.I.C.

Master Bedroom 15⁶x14⁰

Porch

Bedroom No. 2 11⁹x12⁰

Great Room 16⁹x24³

Bedroom No. 3 10⁹x14⁰

Kitchen 12⁶x9⁰

Dining Room 9⁰x16³

Stoop

THIS DESIGN TAKES INSPIRATION from the casual fishing cabins of the Pacific Northwest and interprets it for modern livability. It offers three options for a main entrance. One door opens to a mud porch, where a small hall leads to a galley kitchen and the vaulted great room. Two French doors on the side porch open into a dining room with bay-window seating. Another porch entrance opens directly into the great room, which is centered around a massive stone fireplace and accented with a wall of windows. The secluded master bedroom features a bath with a claw-foot tub and twin pedestal sinks, as well as a separate shower and walk-in closet. Two more bedrooms share a bath. An unfinished loft looks over the great room.

Homes for wide open spaces

DESIGN HPT740040

TOTAL: 3,021 square feet

FIRST FLOOR: 1,924 square feet

SECOND FLOOR: 1,097 square feet

BONUS SPACE: 352 square feet

BEDROOMS: 3

BATHROOMS: 2½

WIDTH: 68'-3" DEPTH: 53'-0"

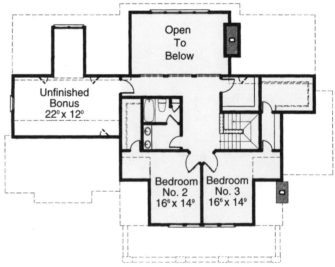

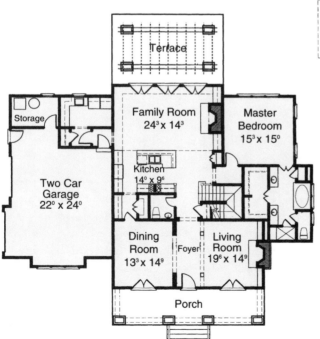

THIS LOVELY CRAFTSMAN-STYLE home invites enjoyment of the outdoors with a front covered porch and a spacious rear terrace. Inside, formal rooms flank the foyer and feature lovely amenities such as French-door access to the front porch. A fireplace warms the family room, which provides plenty of natural light and wide views through three sets of glass doors. Additional bedrooms on the second floor enjoy a balcony overlook to the family room. This home is designed with a basement foundation.

DESIGN HPT740041

TOTAL: 2,204 square feet

FIRST FLOOR: 1,180 square feet

SECOND FLOOR: 1,024 square feet

RECREATION ROOM: 272 square feet

BEDROOMS: 3

BATHROOMS: 2½

WIDTH: 44'-0" DEPTH: 55'-3"

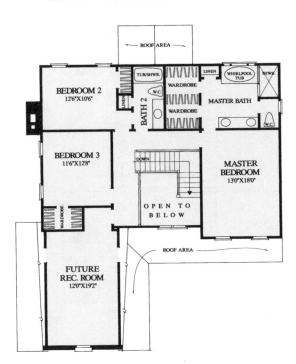

SUGGESTING THE SENTIMENTAL CHARM of the thirties and forties, this three-bedroom home is quaint, charming and affordable. Enter the foyer from the welcoming front porch and entertain guests in the formal living space to the right. The family room and kitchen share an open area at the rear of the plan. Note the sunny breakfast area, large walk-in pantry and cooktop island in the fully functional kitchen. Three bedrooms—one a comfortable master suite—and a future recreation room fill the second floor.

Homes for wide open spaces

DESIGN HPT740042

TOTAL: 4,203 square feet

FIRST FLOOR: 3,120 square feet

SECOND FLOOR: 1,083 square feet

BEDROOMS: 4

BATHROOMS: 5½

WIDTH: 118'-1" DEPTH: 52'-2"

THE BLENDING OF natural materials and a nostalgic farmhouse look gives this home its unique character. Inside, a sophisticated floor plan includes all the amenities demanded by today's upscale family. Three large covered porches, one on the front and two on the rear, provide outdoor entertaining areas. The kitchen features a built-in stone fireplace visible from the breakfast and sun rooms. The master suite includes a large sitting area and a luxurious bath. Upstairs, two additional bedrooms and a large game room will please family and guests. Please specify crawlspace or slab foundation when ordering.

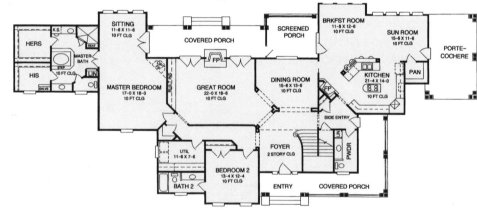

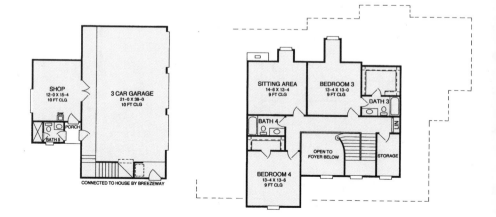

DESIGN HPT740043

TOTAL: 2,495 square feet

FIRST FLOOR: 1,428 square feet

SECOND FLOOR: 1,067 square feet

BONUS SPACE: 342 square feet

BEDROOMS: 3

BATHROOMS: 2½

WIDTH: 74'-0" DEPTH: 64'-8"

EYE-CATCHING TWIN CHIMNEYS

dominate the exterior of this grand design, but on closer approach you will delight in the covered porch with decorated pediment and the tall windows across the front of the house. A long hallway separates the family room, with a fireplace, from the rest of the house. A large U-shaped kitchen features an island work center and direct access to the sunny breakfast room and the formal dining room. A study/living room (with an optional second fireplace) completes the first floor. Upstairs, you'll find a well-appointed master suite, two family bedrooms and a bonus room over the garage.

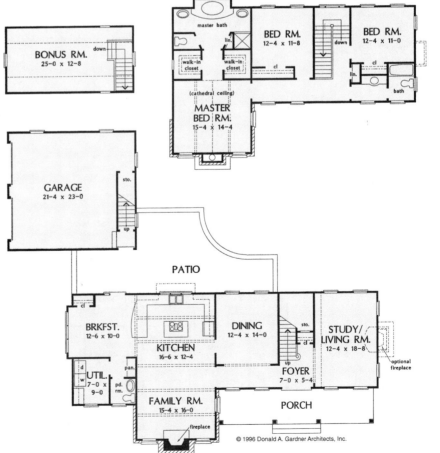

Homes for wide open spaces

DESIGN HPT740044

TOTAL: 2,252 square feet

FIRST FLOOR: 1,736 square feet

SECOND FLOOR: 516 square feet

BONUS SPACE: 272 square feet

BEDROOMS: 3

BATHROOMS: 3

WIDTH: 80'-0" DEPTH: 59'-0"

TWIN MATCHING GABLES set behind the wraparound porch of this three-bedroom home emphasize its country feel. A formal dining room and a study—or make it a fourth bedroom—open to the foyer from the left and right. A hearthwarmed family room sits directly ahead from the entry. Note the screened porch that opens from the family room—perfect for keeping the bugs away on summer days. An amenity filled master suite resides to the right of the family room. Two secondary bedrooms and an optional gameroom complete the second floor.

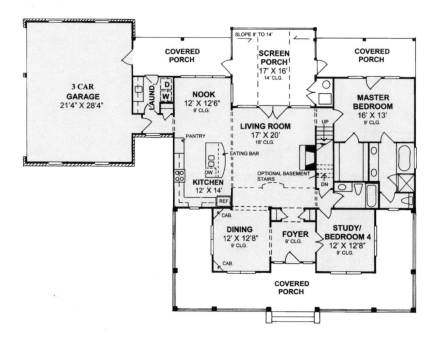

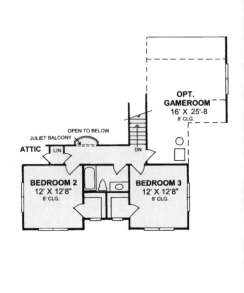

© 1990 Donald A. Gardner Architects, Inc.

DESIGN HPT740045

TOTAL: 2,218 square feet

FIRST FLOOR: 1,651 square feet

SECOND FLOOR: 567 square feet

BEDROOMS: 3

BATHROOMS: 2½

WIDTH: 55'-0" DEPTH: 53'-10"

Quote One®

Cost to build? See page 214
to order complete cost estimate
to build this house in your area!

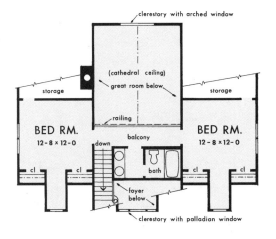

clerestory with arched window

storage

(cathedral ceiling)

great room below

railing

storage

BED RM.
12-8 × 12-0

balcony

BED RM.
12-8 × 12-0

cl   cl

down

bath

cl   cl

foyer
below

clerestory with palladian window

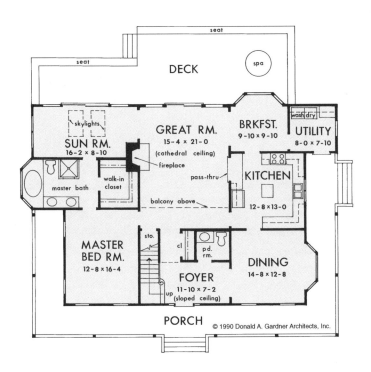

seat

DECK

spa

seat

skylights

SUN RM.
16-2 × 8-10

master bath

walk-in closet

GREAT RM.
15-4 × 21-0
(cathedral ceiling)

fireplace

pass-thru

balcony above

BRKFST.
9-10 × 9-10

wash dry

UTILITY
8-0 × 7-10

KITCHEN
12-8 × 13-0

MASTER
BED RM.
12-8 × 16-4

sto.

cl

p.d.
rm.

FOYER
11-10 × 7-2
(sloped ceiling)

up

DINING
14-8 × 12-8

PORCH

© 1990 Donald A. Gardner Architects, Inc.

A WONDERFUL WRAPAROUND covered porch at
the front and sides of this house and the open deck with a spa at the
back provide plenty of outside living area. Inside, the spacious great
room is appointed with a fireplace, cathedral ceiling and clerestory
with an arched window. The kitchen is centrally located for maximum
flexibility in layout and features a food-preparation island for convenience.
Besides the master bedroom with access to the sun room, there are
two second-level bedrooms that share a full bath.

Homes for wide open spaces

DESIGN HPT740046

TOTAL: 3,007 square feet

FIRST FLOOR: 2,236 square feet

SECOND FLOOR: 771 square feet

BONUS SPACE: 275 square feet

BEDROOMS: 3

BATHROOMS: 2½

WIDTH: 76'-0" **DEPTH:** 62'-3"

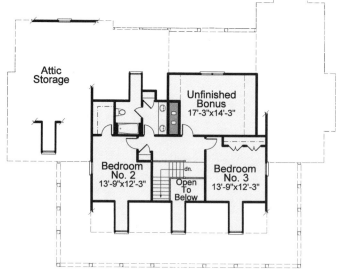

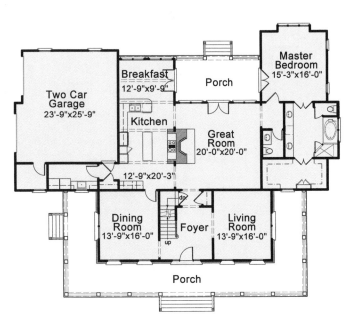

A NEIGHBORLY PORCH EMBRACES three sides of this comfortable home, extending a hearty welcome from its inviting entrance to its warm country kitchen. Inside, rooms open directly onto one another, preserving an old-fashioned farmhouse atmosphere. A soaring, two-story foyer separates the formal living and dining rooms. Openings on both sides of a warming fireplace in the great room lead to a country kitchen where a range top set into a brick chimney arch recalls cooking on an old-time hearth. A sun drenched breakfast area and an expansive master suite that features a box-bay window and a sumptuous bath bracket the rear porch. Upstairs, dormers accent two family bedrooms and a shared bath, while bonus space can easily become a third bedroom or a convenient home office. This home is designed with a basement foundation.

DESIGN HPT740047

TOTAL: 2,357 square feet

FIRST FLOOR: 1,492 square feet

SECOND FLOOR: 865 square feet

GAME ROOM: 285 square feet

BEDROOMS: 4

BATHROOMS: 3½

WIDTH: 66'-10" **DEPTH:** 49'-7"

THIS ROOMY, QUINTESSENTIAL country design features two covered porches and an island kitchen with a breakfast area. The long foyer leads to the living room with a fireplace and to the stunning master suite with an oversized tub, glass shower and twin walk-in closets. A balcony overlooks the spectacular living area and leads to three additional bedrooms and two full baths. The two-car garage includes storage space and a side entrance. Please specify crawlspace or slab foundation when ordering.

Homes for wide open spaces

DESIGN HPT740048

SQUARE FOOTAGE: 2,449

FUTURE SPACE: 921 square feet

BEDROOMS: 3

BATHROOMS: 2½

WIDTH: 85'-8" DEPTH: 70'-7"

NOSTALGIC IN EVERY WAY, this American farmhouse is reminiscent of the homes that dotted the countryside in the late 1800's. Inside, an updated floor plan makes this a pleasing layout for today's owner. Designed for the growing family, this home features an expandable second floor with room to add a bedroom, a bath, and a game room. Downstairs, elegant arches open to the large great room and dining room. Nine-foot ceilings are used throughout the first floor to give the home a spacious feeling. Please specify crawlspace or slab foundation when ordering.

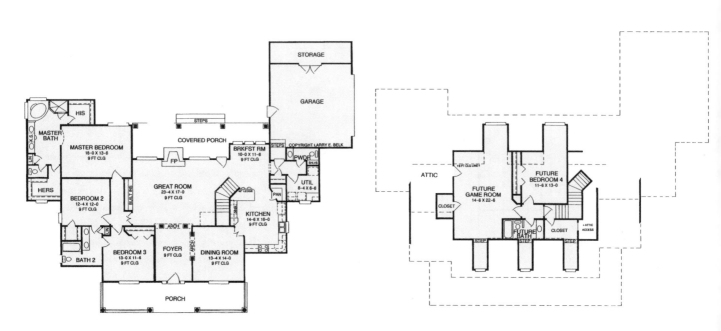

DESIGN HPT740049

SQUARE FOOTAGE: 2,002

BEDROOMS: 3

BATHROOMS: 2

WIDTH: 66'-0" **DEPTH:** 60'-0"

A RAISED FRONT PORCH, charming transoms over multi-pane windows and a French-door entry earmark this three-bedroom home with country charisma. Natural light floods the hearth-warmed living room from a skylight above and from doors to the front and rear porches. To the left of the entry, the formal dining room features built-in shelves and easy access to the kitchen. An angled serving bar connects the kitchen with the bayed, informal eating area. Secluded to the rear of the house, the master bedroom awaits, with its luxurious bath and private office. The office includes a separate entrance and a built-in desk. Two family bedrooms share a full bath to the right of the plan. Please specify crawlspace or slab foundation when ordering.

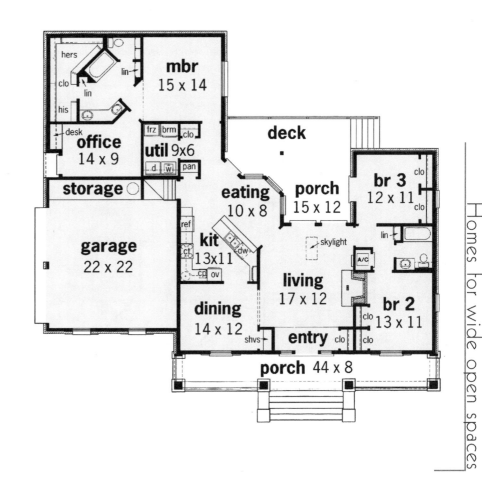

Homes for wide open spaces

DESIGN HPT740050

SQUARE FOOTAGE: 2,636

BEDROOMS: 4

BATHROOMS: 3

WIDTH: 96'-6" DEPTH: 52'-4"

THIS HOME MAKES A commanding presence with its country porch and stone veneer accents. Upon entering, views throughout the home are possible as this home reaches out in all directions. The living room has a wall of glass to the covered patio, and the dining room, with its decorative columns and angular wall, creates an impressive space. The master suite is welcomed through double doors with a decorative niche nearby. The family living area of this home is just as impressive, with a massive island kitchen serving as the centerpiece. The generous nook can accommodate a large family, as can the family room with its a media/fireplace wall.

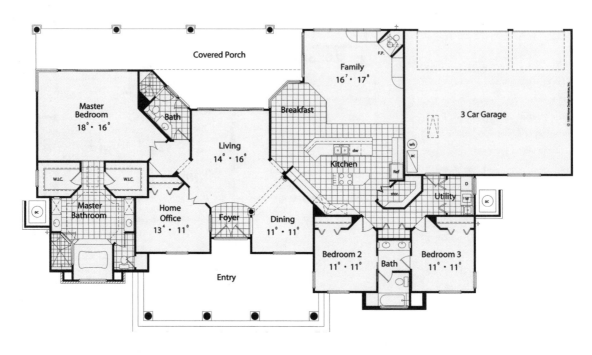

DESIGN HPT740051

SQUARE FOOTAGE: 1,974

BEDROOMS: 3

BATHROOMS: 2

WIDTH: 56'-0" DEPTH: 58'-4"

WITH A STONE and stucco exterior, this craftsman style home is solid inside and out. Tray ceilings accent both the dining and great rooms. Amenities such as a fireplace and a pass-through to the kitchen will enhance the comfort of the great room. Access the rear porch from the great room, breakfast area and one of the family bedrooms. A spacious and luxurious master suite fills the right side of the plan while the two family bedrooms share a full bath to the left.

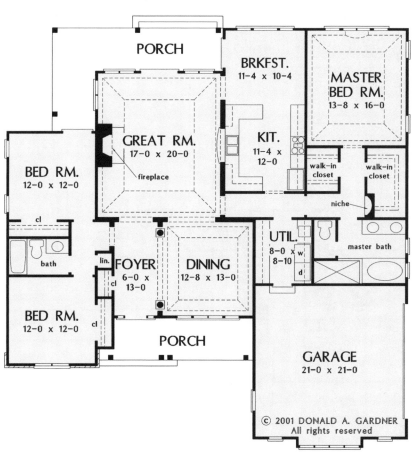

Homes for wide open spaces

DESIGN HPT740052

SQUARE FOOTAGE: 2,102

BONUS SPACE: 351 square feet

BEDROOMS: 3

BATHROOMS: 2

WIDTH: 75'-0" **DEPTH:** 44'-8"

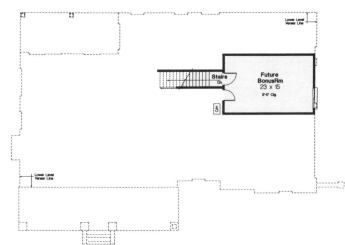

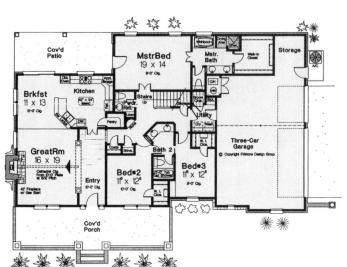

PRIVACY, COMFORT AND convience is each household members advantage in this home. Two family bedrooms enjoy walk-in closets and personal access to a full bath with dual vanities. The master bedroom opens through double doors and provides a luxurious master bath with a whirpool tub, compartmented toilet and an over-sized walk-in closet. In the island kitchen is a large pantry for added space and a snack bar that divides the breakfast area. The great room is defined by columns and displays a fireplace. Additional storage space is located in the three-car garage.

DESIGN HPT740053

TOTAL: 2,438 square feet

FIRST FLOOR: 1,900 square feet

SECOND FLOOR: 538 square feet

BONUS SPACE: 302 square feet

BEDROOMS: 4

BATHROOMS: 3

WIDTH: 79'-0" DEPTH: 59'-0"

INSIDE THIS TWO-STORY retreat are three family bedrooms and a first-floor master bedroom. The master bedroom pleases with access to the screened porch, a full private bath with a walk-in closet. Two family bedrooms are upstairs with a full hall bath and an optional game room, while the fourth bedroom/study, remains secluded on the first floor. The dining room is just beyond the entry; the cooktop island kitchen and nook area are nearby. The living room succeeds at offering the ultimate comfort with a fireplace and double doors to the screened porch where the morning sun will be enjoyed.

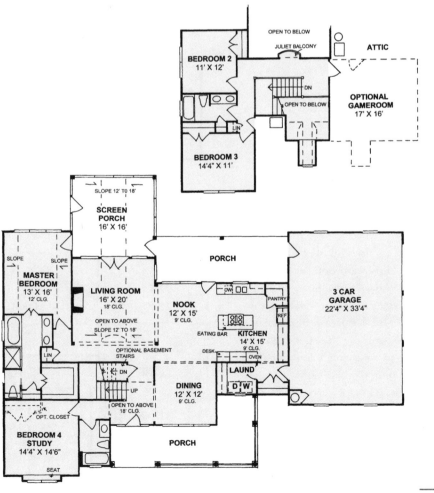

Homes for wide open spaces

©1999 Donald A. Gardner, Inc.

B. NATHAN

DESIGN HPT740054

SQUARE FOOTAGE: 2,078

BONUS SPACE: 339 square feet

BEDROOMS: 3

BATHROOMS: 2½

WIDTH: 62'-2" DEPTH: 47'-8"

AN ENCHANTING L-SHAPED front porch lends charm and grace to this country home with dual dormers and gables. Bay windows expand both of the home's dining areas, while the great room and kitchen are amplified by a shared cathedral ceiling. The generous great room features a fireplace with flanking built-ins, skylights and access to a marvelous back porch. A cathedral ceiling enhances the master suite, which enjoys a large walk-in closet and a luxurious bath. Two more bedrooms share a generous hall bath that has a dual-sink vanity.

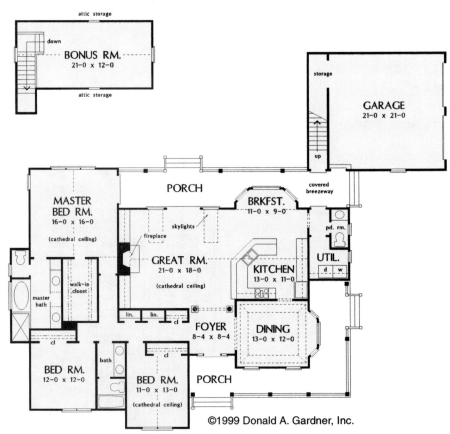

©1999 Donald A. Gardner, Inc.

DESIGN HPT740055

SQUARE FOOTAGE: 2,546

GAME ROOM: 407 square feet

BEDROOMS: 4

BATHROOMS: 2½

WIDTH: 74'-0" **DEPTH:** 74'-0"

THE WRAPAROUND PORCH of this decidedly country farmhouse nearly envelopes the entire home, with a screened porch in the rear sectioning off a private porch for the master suite. The well-equipped kitchen is neatly placed between the sunny breakfast nook, the elegant living room and the formal dining room. The master suite boasts two walk-in closets, twin vanities and a compartmented toilet. The family bedrooms are situated on the far right with a shared full bath. The second floors holds space available for future development.

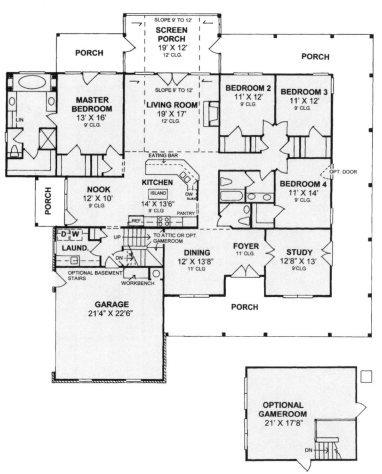

DESIGN HPT740056

SQUARE FOOTAGE: 1,761

BEDROOMS: 4

BATHROOMS: 2

WIDTH: 57'-0" DEPTH: 52'-2"

RESIDING PEACEFULLY in a serene mountain setting, this small family home brings quaint style to an efficient floor plan. The covered porch leads inside to formal vistas from the dining and great rooms. Warmed by a cozy fireplace, the vaulted great room connects to the kitchen/breakfast area, opening onto a rear patio. The master bedroom is vaulted and includes a walk-in closet and private bath. Three additional family bedrooms share a full hall bath. A two-car garage completes this charming plan.

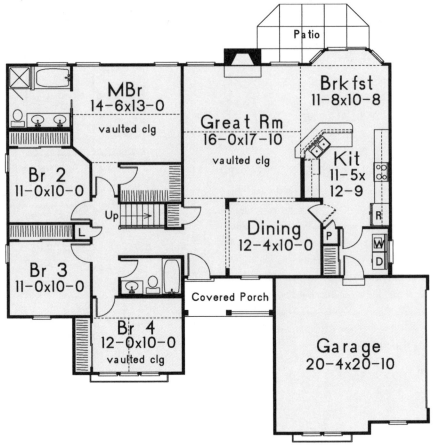

© 1994 Donald A. Gardner Architects, Inc.

B. NATHAN

DESIGN HPT740057

SQUARE FOOTAGE: 2,207

BONUS SPACE: 435 square feet

BEDROOMS: 3

BATHROOMS: 2½

WIDTH: 76'-1" DEPTH: 50'-0"

THIS QUAINT FOUR-BEDROOM HOME with front and rear porches reinforces its beauty with arched windows and dormers. The pillared dining room opens on the right, while a study that could double as a guest room is available on the left. Straight ahead lies the massive great room with its cathedral ceiling, enchanting fireplace and access to the private rear porch. Within steps of the dining room is the efficient kitchen and the sunny breakfast nook. The master suite enjoys a cathedral ceiling, rear-deck access and a master bath with a skylit whirlpool tub. Three additional bedrooms located at the opposite end of the house share a full bath.

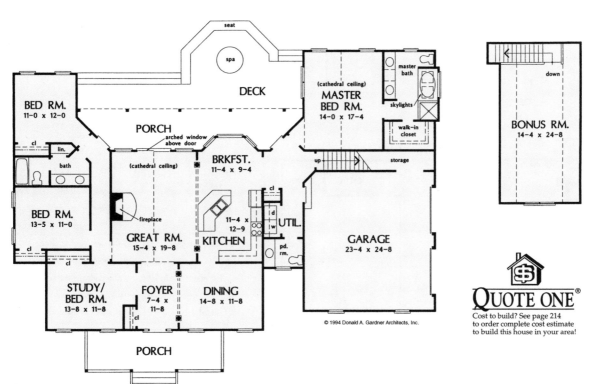

seat

spa

DECK

BED RM.
11-0 x 12-0

PORCH

cl lin.

bath

(cathedral ceiling)

arched window
above door

BRKFST.
11-4 x 9-4

master
bath

skylights

(cathedral ceiling)

MASTER
BED RM.
14-0 x 17-4

walk-in
closet

BED RM.
13-5 x 11-0

fireplace

11-4 x
12-9

d
w

cl

up

storage

BONUS RM.
14-4 x 24-8

down

GREAT RM.
15-4 x 19-8

KITCHEN

UTIL.

pd.
rm.

GARAGE
23-4 x 24-8

STUDY/
BED RM.
13-8 x 11-8

FOYER
7-4 x
11-8

cl

DINING
14-8 x 11-8

© 1994 Donald A. Gardner Architects, Inc.

PORCH

Homes for wide open spaces

© 1998   Donald A Gardner, Inc.

DESIGN HPT740058

TOTAL: 2,251 square feet

FIRST FLOOR: 1,569 square feet

SECOND FLOOR: 682 square feet

BONUS SPACE: 332 square feet

BEDROOMS: 3

BATHROOMS: 2½

WIDTH: 64'-8" **DEPTH:** 43'-4"

© 1998   Donald A Gardner, Inc.

THE WIDE PORCH ACROSS the front and the deck off the great room in back allow as much outdoor living as the weather permits. The foyer opens through columns off the front porch to the dining room, with a nearby powder room, and to the great room. The breakfast room is open to the great room and the adjacent kitchen. The utility room adjoins this area and accesses the garage. On the opposite side of the plan, the master suite offers a compartmented bath and two walk-in closets. A staircase leads upstairs to two family bedrooms—one at each end of a balcony that overlooks the great room. Each bedroom contains a walk-in closet, a dormer window and private access to the bath through a private vanity area.

66

DESIGN HPT740059

TOTAL: 1,692 square feet

FIRST FLOOR: 847 square feet

SECOND FLOOR: 845 square feet

BEDROOMS: 3

BATHROOMS: 2½

WIDTH: 27'-0" DEPTH: 61'-0"

THIS PETITE BUNGALOW is perfect for narrow lots and still provides plenty of amenities for the whole family. The entry opens directly into the vaulted great room. Here, a wood stove, built-ins and an adjacent, vaulted dining room provide fantastic ambience. The C-shaped kitchen features a sink overlooking the great room, a pantry and plenty of counter and cabinet space. A nearby nook offers outdoor access and built-in shelves. Upstairs, the master suite is designed with a private balcony, a walk-in closet and a full bath. Two secondary bedrooms share a full hall bath that includes a dual-bowl vanity.

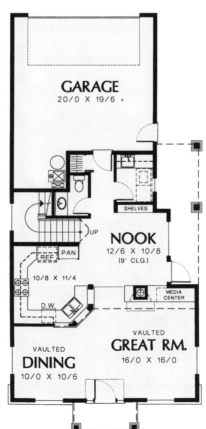

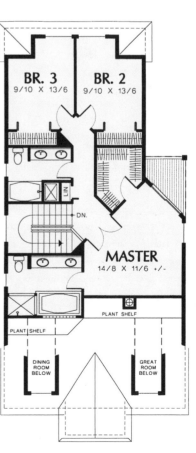

© 1997 Donald A Gardner Architects, Inc.

DESIGN HPT740060

TOTAL: 1,669 square feet

FIRST FLOOR: 1,219 square feet

SECOND FLOOR: 450 square feet

BONUS SPACE: 406 square feet

BEDROOMS: 3

BATHROOMS: 2½

WIDTH: 50'-4"   DEPTH: 49'-2"

THIS THREE-BEDROOM narrow-lot home offers some of the extras usually reserved for wider lots, such as a wraparound porch and a two-car garage. A vaulted ceiling adds volume to the great room, while columns and a bay window add distinction to the dining room. The kitchen is designed for efficiency and offers access to the side porch and rear deck for outdoor dining options. The master bedrooms sits behind the two-car garage to shield it from noise while two family bedrooms, a full bath and the bonus room reside upstairs. The large bonus room can be adapted to serve additional family needs.

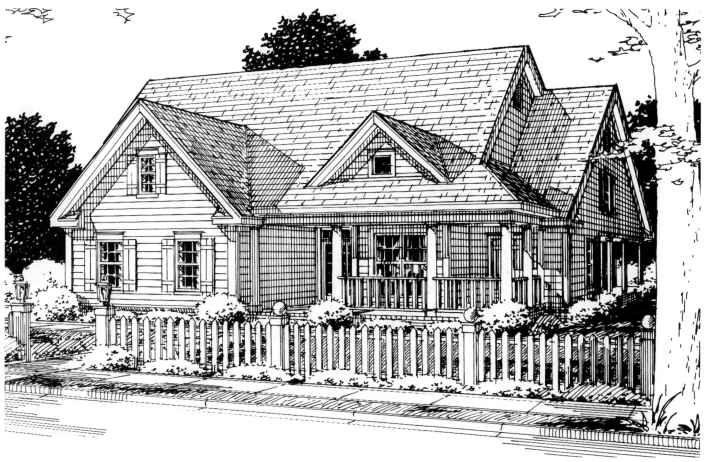

DESIGN HPT740061

SQUARE FOOTAGE: 1,842

GAME ROOM: 386 square feet

BEDROOMS: 3

BATHROOMS: 2

WIDTH: 54'-0" DEPTH: 63'-0"

A WRAPAROUND front porch and an interesting roofline add style to this efficient country cottage that boasts a total of four covered porches. The foyer opens to the living room with a corner fireplace and two walls of windows. Just past the snack bar of the island kitchen is the formal dining room that opens to the vaulted screen porch. The master suite is tucked behind the kitchen for privacy while two family bedrooms sit to the right of the foyer where they share a full bath.

OPTIONAL GAMEROOM
20'4" X 16'

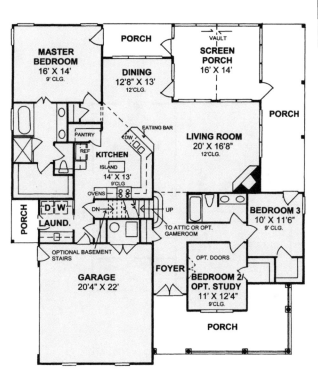

MASTER BEDROOM
16' X 14'
9' CLG.

PORCH

DINING
12'8" X 13'
12'CLG.

SCREEN PORCH
16' X 14'

VAULT

PORCH

PANTRY

EATIING BAR

LIVING ROOM
20' X 16'8"
12'CLG.

REF

KITCHEN

DW

ISLAND
14' X 13'
9'CLG

OVENS

PORCH

D W
LAUND.

DN

UP

TO ATTIC OR OPT.
GAMEROOM

BEDROOM 3
10' X 11'6"
9' CLG.

OPTIONAL BASEMENT STAIRS

GARAGE
20'4" X 22'

FOYER

OPT. DOORS

BEDROOM 2/
OPT. STUDY
11' X 12'4"
9'CLG.

PORCH

DESIGN HPT740062

SQUARE FOOTAGE: 1,583 square feet

BONUS SPACE: 284 square feet

OPTIONAL BEDROOM: 248 square feet

BEDROOMS: 3

BATHROOMS: 2

WIDTH: 54'-0" DEPTH: 47'-6"

THIS COMFORTABLE COTTAGE is well suited to an alpine environment, yet, with a flexible interior and superior architecture, will build anywhere. Open living and dining space is anchored by a decorative column and a fireplace surrounded by views. A well-planned kitchen features a food-preparation island and a serving bar. A triple window in the breakfast area brightens the kitchen, while a French door allows access to the rear property. To the right of the plan, the master suite boasts a vaulted bath, a plant shelf and a walk-in closet. Two secondary bedrooms share a full bath. Please specify basement or crawlspace foundation when ordering.

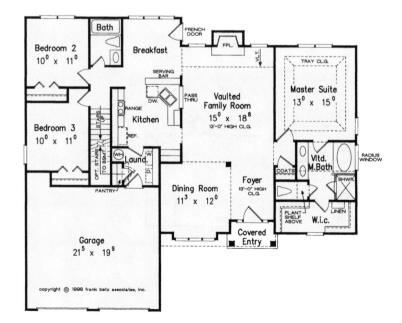

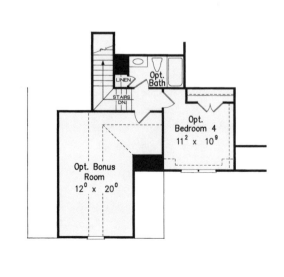

DESIGN HPT740063

SQUARE FOOTAGE: 2,170

BEDROOMS: 3

BATHROOMS: 3

WIDTH: 62'-0" **DEPTH:** 61'-6"

THIS CLASSIC COTTAGE features a stone and wooden exterior with an arch-detailed porch and a box-bay window. From a hallway off the foyer, double doors open to the den with built-in bookcases and a fireplace. A full bath is situated next to the den, allowing for an optional guest room. The family room is centrally located, just beyond the foyer. Its hearth is framed by windows overlooking the porch at the rear of the home. A breakfast area complements the attractive and efficiently designed kitchen. The master bedroom includes a private bath with a large walk-in closet, double vanities, a corner tub and separate shower. Two secondary bedrooms with large closets share a full bath featuring double vanities. This home is designed with a walkout basement foundation.

QUOTE ONE®
Cost to build? See page 214
to order complete cost estimate
to build this house in your area!

Homes for wide open spaces

© 1999 Donald A. Gardner, Inc.+

DESIGN HPT740064

SQUARE FOOTAGE: 1,971

BONUS SPACE: 358 square feet

BEDROOMS: 3

BATHROOMS: 3

WIDTH: 62'-6" DEPTH: 57'-2"

THIS CRAFTSMAN COTTAGE combines stone, siding, and cedar shakes to create striking curb appeal. The interior features an open floor plan with high ceilings, columns and bay windows to visually expand space. Built-in cabinetry, a fireplace and a kitchen pass-through both highlight and add convenience to the great room. The master suite features a tray ceiling in the bedroom and a bath with garden tub, separate shower, dual vanities and a walk-in closet. On the opposite side of the home an additional bedroom could be used as a second master suite, and above the garage, a bonus room provides ample storage and room to grow.

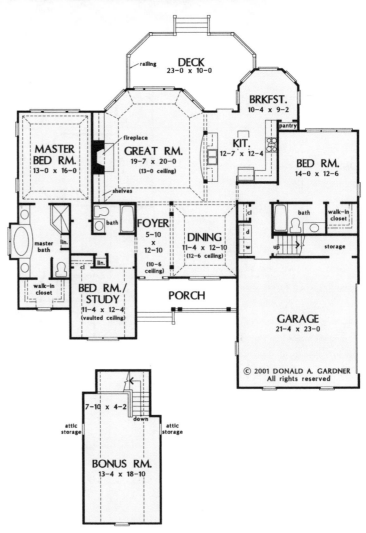

DON'T LET A SLOPED LOT deter you from getting the plan you want. This grand home accommodates a side slope without losing any livability. The lower level has a two-car garage and a storage area or bonus space. On the main level, the great room and dining room are open and divided only by two decorative columns. A nearby nook and gallery kitchen have access to a rear deck. for quieter times, the den sits to the right of the foyer. Three bedrooms include two family bedrooms with shared bath and a master suite. Look for a spa tub, walk-in closet and tray ceiling in the master suite.

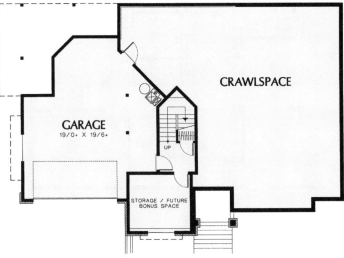

DESIGN HPT740065

SQUARE FOOTAGE: 2,124

LOWER ENTRY: 112 square feet

BEDROOMS: 3

BATHROOMS: 2

WIDTH: 61'-0" DEPTH: 45'-0"

Homes for wide open spaces

DESIGN HPT740066

SQUARE FOOTAGE: 1,244

BEDROOMS: 3

BATHROOMS: 2

WIDTH: 44'-0" **DEPTH:** 62'-0"

COME HOME TO the relaxed country style of this three-bedroom plan. A beautiful porch adorns the entire length of the front of the house—perfect for hanging plants. The entry opens directly to the hearth-warmed living room with built-in bookshelves and a wood box. The dining room sits open to the living room and the U-shaped kitchen, and features convenient access to the carport. To the right of the plan reside three bedrooms. Two family bedrooms share a full hall bath, while the master bedroom enjoys a private bath. Please specify crawlspace or slab foundation when ordering.

DESIGN HPT740067

TOTAL: 1,938 square feet

FIRST FLOOR: 1,044 square feet

SECOND FLOOR: 894 square feet

BONUS SPACE: 228 square feet

BEDROOMS: 3

BATHROOMS: 2½

WIDTH: 58'-0" **DEPTH:** 43'-6"

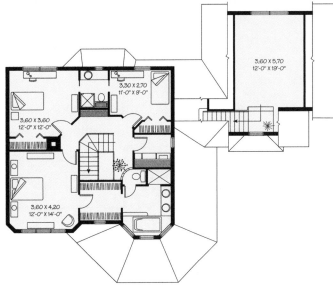

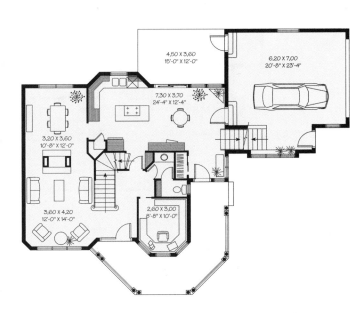

THIS CHARMING COUNTRY traditional home provides a well-lit home office, harbored in a beautiful bay with three windows. The second-floor bay brightens the master bath, which has a double-bowl vanity, a step-up tub and a dressing area. The living and dining rooms share a two-sided fireplace. The gourmet kitchen has a cooktop island counter and enjoys outdoor views through sliding glass doors in the breakfast area. A sizable bonus room above the two-car garage can be developed into hobby space or a recreation room. This home is designed with a basement foundation.

THIS ELEGANT VICTORIAN FEATURES an exterior of distinctive decorative detailing, yet offers an interior plan that satisfies today's standards. A spacious living room incorporates a large bay-windowed area and a fireplace. The generous kitchen with island counter is centrally located to the dining and family rooms and to the sun room. On the second level, the master suite has a fireplace, walk-in closet and bay-windowed area which can serve as a study. Of the three additional bedrooms, one enjoys a private bath; the others share a full bath.

DESIGN HPT740068

TOTAL: 2,588 square feet
FIRST FLOOR: 1,393 square feet
SECOND FLOOR: 1,195 square feet
BEDROOMS: 4
BATHROOMS: 3½
WIDTH: 44'-0" DEPTH: 50'-8"

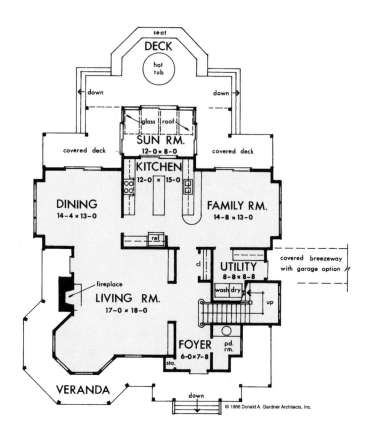

DESIGN HPT740069

TOTAL: 1,801 square feet

FIRST FLOOR: 960 square feet

SECOND FLOOR: 841 square feet

BEDROOMS: 3

BATHROOMS: 1½

WIDTH: 36'-0"   **DEPTH:** 30'-0"

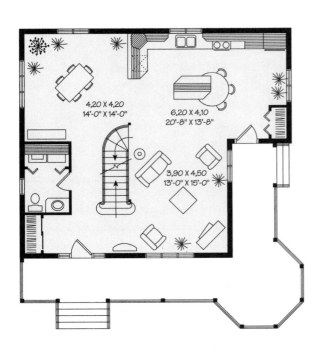

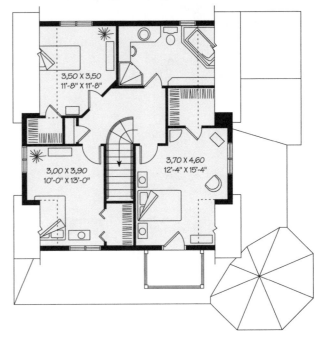

THIS ROMANTIC COTTAGE DESIGN is ideal for any countryside setting. Lively Victorian details enhance the exterior. A wrapping porch with a gazebo-style sitting area encourages refreshing outdoor relaxation, while interior spaces are open to each other. The kitchen with a snack bar is open to both the dining area and the living room area. A powder bath with laundry facilities completes the first floor. The second floor offers space for three family bedrooms with walk-in closets and a pampering whirlpool bath. This home is designed with a basement foundation.

DESIGN HPT740070

TOTAL: 2,040 square feet

FIRST FLOOR: 1,070 square feet

SECOND FLOOR: 970 square feet

BEDROOMS: 3

BATHROOMS: 1½

WIDTH: 36'-0" **DEPTH:** 38'-0"

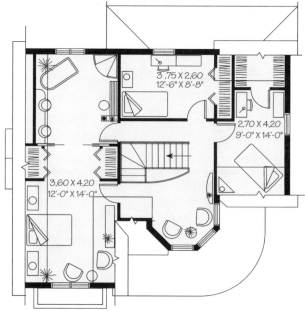

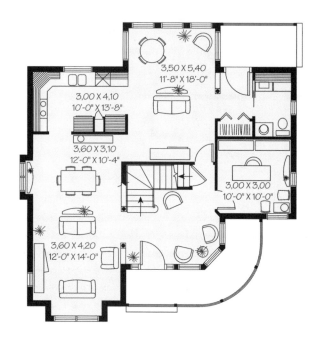

VICTORIAN STYLING can come in an affordable size, as this home shows. A sitting area inside the front hall connects with the family room for handling large parties. An enclosed room off the sitting area can be used as a study or extra bedroom. A combination half-bath and laundry is just inside the rear entrance for quick cleanup; the covered rear porch is accessed from a door just beyond the laundry area. For easy upkeep, the three bedrooms on the second floor share a full bath that includes a corner tub. One of the bedrooms offers access to a private balcony. This home is designed with a basement foundation.

DESIGN HPT740071

TOTAL: 2,820 square feet

FIRST FLOOR: 1,632 square feet

SECOND FLOOR: 1,188 square feet

BEDROOMS: 3

BATHROOMS: 2½

WIDTH: 61'-3" **DEPTH:** 68'-6"

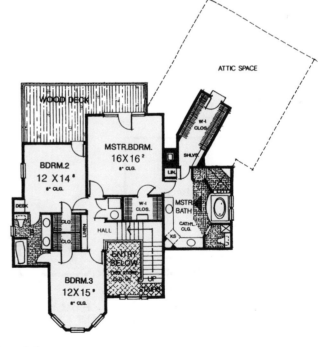

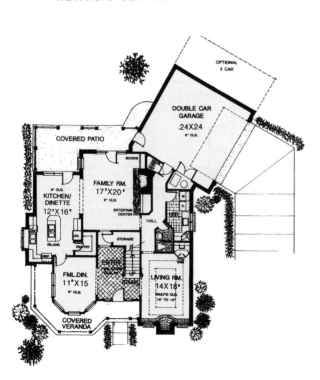

THIS VICTORIAN FARMHOUSE is distinct because of its ornate detailing, including the decorative pinnacle, covered porch and front-facing chimney. The living room is graced with a fireplace, wet bar and vaulted ceiling. The family room also includes some appreciated amenities: an entertainment center, built-in bookshelves and access to the covered patio. Upstairs, both the master suite and Bedroom 2 easily access the deck, and all bedrooms sport spacious walk-in closets. Ample attic space is also available for storage.

DESIGN HPT740072

TOTAL: 1,872 square feet

FIRST FLOOR: 1,320 square feet

SECOND FLOOR: 552 square feet

BEDROOMS: 3

BATHROOMS: 4

WIDTH: 56'-0" DEPTH: 61'-0"

THIS UNIQUE ROOFING STYLE captures your attention and the varying rooflines hold your interest. The foyer is open to the dining room on the left and the living room on the right. A large family room is straight ahead, featuring a built-in bookshelf and fireplace. The efficient kitchen offers plenty of counter space in a relatively small area. A wall of windows in the eating room allows light to billow into this home. The master suite includes a bath and walk-in closets. Large front and rear porches provide extensive opportunity for outdoor entertaining. Please specify basement, crawlspace or slab foundation when ordering.

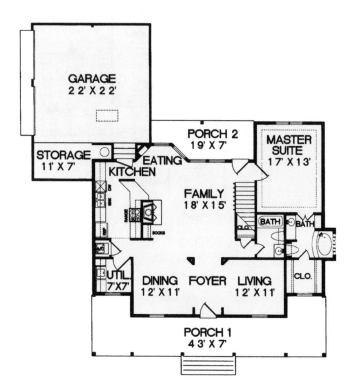

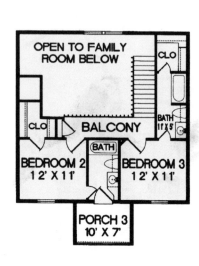

DESIGN HPT740073

SQUARE FOOTAGE: 2,502

BEDROOMS: 3

BATHROOMS: 2

WIDTH: 70'-0" DEPTH: 72'-0"

COTTAGE QUAINTNESS and Victorian accents lend a timeless style to this family design. The covered front entry porch welcomes you inside to a foyer that's open to a combined living room/dining area, defined by columns. Two sets of double doors open to the expansive rear porch. The kitchen, open to the dining room, features an island workstation and a casual breakfast nook. Two family bedrooms share a hall bath with the quiet office/study. The master suite provides private access to the rear porch, His and Hers walk-in closets and a spacious bath.

DESIGN HPT740074

TOTAL: 2,272 square feet
FIRST FLOOR: 1,572 square feet
SECOND FLOOR: 700 square feet
BONUS SPACE: 212 square feet
BEDROOMS: 4
BATHROOMS: 2½
WIDTH: 70'-0" **DEPTH:** 38'-5"

COUNTRY AND VICTORIAN ELEMENTS give this home a down-home feel. A charming porch wraps around the front of this farmhouse, whose entry opens to a formal dining room. The island kitchen and sun-filled breakfast area are located nearby. The family room is warmed by a fireplace flanked by windows. Located for privacy, the first-floor master bedroom features its own covered patio and a private bath designed for relaxation. The second floor contains three family bedrooms—each with a walk-in closet—a full bath and a future bonus room.

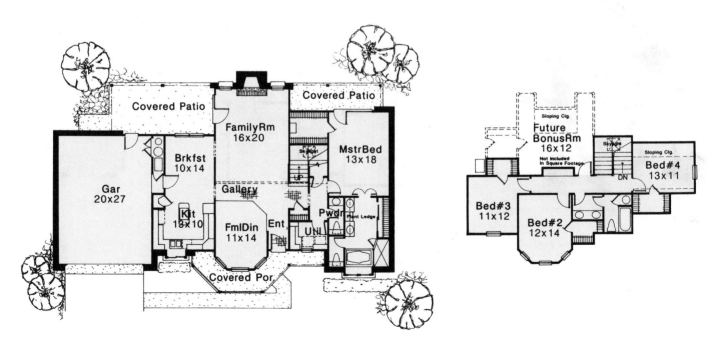

DESIGN HPT740075

TOTAL: 2,586 square feet

FIRST FLOOR: 2,028 square feet

SECOND FLOOR: 558 square feet

BONUS SPACE: 272 square feet

BEDROOMS: 4

BATHROOMS: 3

WIDTH: 64'-10" **DEPTH:** 61'-0"

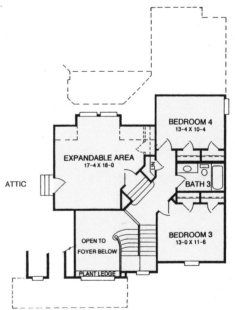

DOUBLE COLUMNS and an arch-top clerestory window create an inviting entry to this fresh interpretation of Colonial style. The two-story foyer features a decorative ledge—perfect for displaying a tapestry. Decorative columns and arches open to the formal dining room and to the octagonal great room, which provides a ten-foot tray ceiling. The kitchen looks over an angled counter to a breakfast bay that brings in the outdoors and shares a through-fireplace with the great room. Please specify basement, crawlspace or slab foundation when ordering.

DESIGN HPT740076

TOTAL: 2,126 square feet

FIRST FLOOR: 1,583 square feet

SECOND FLOOR: 543 square feet

BONUS SPACE: 251 square feet

BEDROOMS: 4

BATHROOMS: 3

WIDTH: 53'-0" DEPTH: 47'-0"

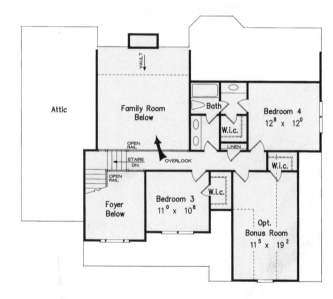

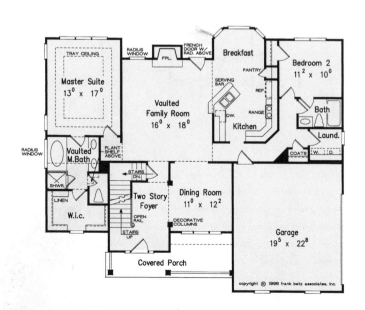

HERE'S A NEW COUNTRY home with a fresh face and a dash of Victoriana. Inside, decorative columns help define an elegant dining room, but the heart of the home is the vaulted family room with a radius window and a French door to the rear property. The first-floor master suite features a private bath with a vaulted ceiling and a whirlpool tub set off with a radius window. The second floor boasts two bedrooms—each with walk-in closets—a shared bath and an open hallway that overlooks that family room and foyer below. Please specify basement, slab or crawlspace foundation when ordering.

THIS CHARMING EXTERIOR conceals a perfect family plan. The formal dining and living rooms reside on either side of the foyer. At the rear of the home is a family room with a fireplace and access to a deck and veranda. The modern kitchen features a sunlit breakfast area. The second floor provides four bedrooms, one of which may be finished at a later date and used as a guest suite. The master suite includes a private bath and roomy walk-in closet. Note the extra storage space in the two-car garage. This home is designed with a walkout basement foundation.

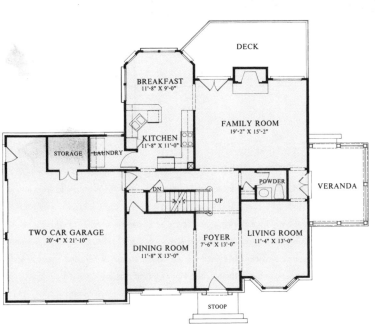

DESIGN HPT740077

TOTAL: 2,365 square feet

FIRST FLOOR: 1,205 square feet

SECOND FLOOR: 1,160 square feet

OPTIONAL BEDROOM: 350 square feet

BEDROOMS: 3

BATHROOMS: 3½

WIDTH: 52'-6" DEPTH: 43'-6"

Cost to build? See page 214 to order complete cost estimate to build this house in your area!

DESIGN HPT740078

TOTAL: 1,818 square feet

FIRST FLOOR: 1,382 square feet

SECOND FLOOR: 436 square feet

BONUS SPACE: 298 square feet

BEDROOMS: 3

BATHROOMS: 2½

WIDTH: 52'-4" DEPTH: 45'-10"

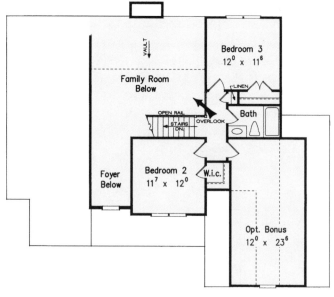

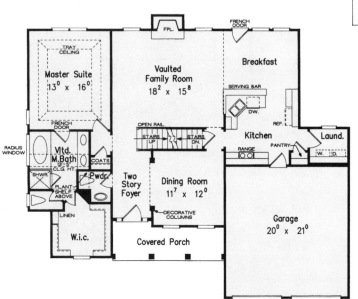

VARIETY IN THE FACADE is just a prelude to the charm to be found inside this attractive three-bedroom home. The two-story foyer opens on the right to a formal dining room, then leads back to a vaulted family room—complete with a warming fireplace. The efficient kitchen offers a breakfast bar and easy access to the breakfast area. The master suite is lavish with its amenities. Included here is a huge walk-in closet, a separate tub and shower, and a tray ceiling in the bedroom. Upstairs, two family bedrooms share a full hall bath. An optional bonus room is available for future development. Please specify basement or crawlspace foundation when ordering.

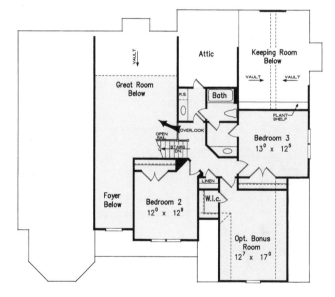

DESIGN HPT740079

TOTAL: 2,551 square feet

FIRST FLOOR: 1,972 square feet

SECOND FLOOR: 579 square feet

BONUS SPACE: 256 square feet

BEDROOMS: 3

BATHROOMS: 2½

WIDTH: 55'-0" DEPTH: 51'-2"

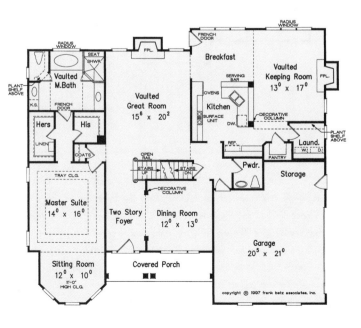

A BEAUTIFUL ONE-STORY TURRET accompanied by arched windows and a stucco facade invite you into this home. A terrific casual combination of kitchen, breakfast area and a vaulted keeping room provide a space for family gatherings. Both the keeping room and great room sport cheery fireplaces. The master suite is secluded on the first floor. This relaxing retreat offers a sitting room, His and Hers walk-in closets, dual vanities and compartmented toilet. Two family bedrooms share a full bath on the second floor. An optional bonus room can be used as a game room or home office. Please specify basement or crawlspace foundation when ordering.

Homes for America's heartland

DESIGN HPT740080

TOTAL: 2,790 square feet

FIRST FLOOR: 1,840 square feet

SECOND FLOOR: 950 square feet

BEDROOMS: 4

BATHROOMS: 3½

WIDTH: 58'-6" DEPTH: 62'-0"

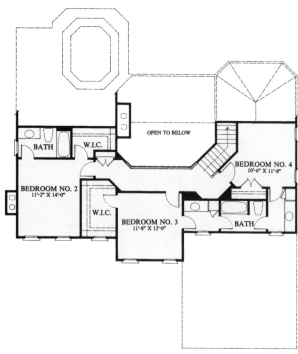

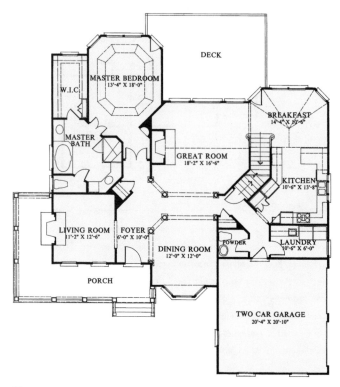

THE APPEARANCE OF THIS EARLY American home brings the past to mind with its wraparound porch, wood siding and flower-box detailing. Inside, columns frame the great room and dining room. Left of the foyer lies the living room with a warming fireplace. The angular kitchen joins a sunny breakfast nook. The master bedroom has a spacious private bath and a walk-in closet. Stairs to the second level lead from the breakfast area to an open landing overlooking the great room. Three family bedrooms—two with walk-in closets and all three with private access to a bath—complete this level. This home is designed with a walkout basement foundation.

DESIGN HPT740081

TOTAL: 3,407 square feet

FIRST FLOOR: 2,384 square feet

SECOND FLOOR: 1,023 square feet

BONUS SPACE: 228 square feet

BEDROOMS: 4

BATHROOMS: 3½

WIDTH: 63'-4" **DEPTH:** 57'-0"

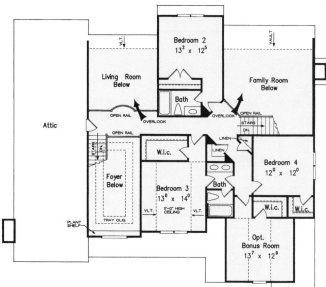

THE COVERED FRONT PORCH of this stucco home opens to a two-story foyer and one of two staircases. Arched openings lead into both the formal dining room and the vaulted living room. The efficient kitchen features a walk-in pantry, built-in desk, work island and separate snack bar. Nearby, the large breakfast area opens to the family room. Lavish in its amenities, the master suite offers a separate, vaulted sitting room with a fireplace, among other luxuries. Three bedrooms, along with optional bonus space and attic storage, are found on the second floor. Please specify basement or crawlspace foundation when ordering.

Homes for America's heartland

DESIGN HPT740082

SQUARE FOOTAGE: 2,135

OPTIONAL GAME ROOM: 315 square feet

BEDROOMS: 3

BATHROOMS: 2½

WIDTH: 84'-0" **DEPTH:** 62'-6"

THE PEDIMENT OVER the front entry, flanked by twin dormers, adds a hint of Southern hospitality to this three-bedroom home. The island kitchen is conveniently located to serve any occassion—hors d'oeuvres in the living room, brunch in the breakfast nook or dinner in the formal dining room. The screened porch connects the two covered porches at the rear. The bedrooms are split for privacy, putting the lavish master suite on the left with access to the rear. An optional game room is available for future development.

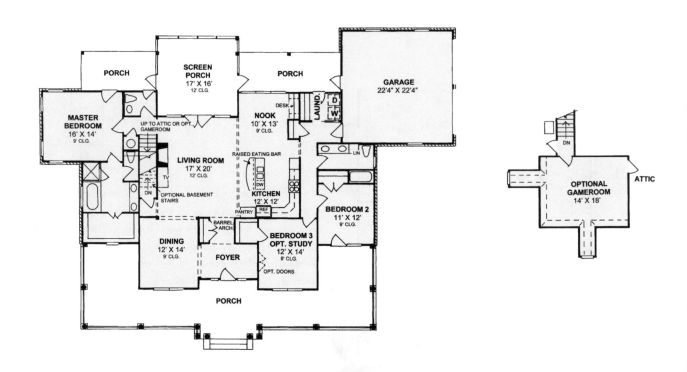

DESIGN HPT740083

SQUARE FOOTAGE: 1,604

BONUS SPACE: 316 square feet

BEDROOMS: 3

BATHROOMS: 2

WIDTH: 57'-0" DEPTH: 59'-0"

THIS TRADITIONAL COTTAGE PLAN offers a simple one-story design with a bonus room for flexible use. A wrapping front porch welcomes you inside to a formal living room warmed by a fireplace. The island kitchen is open to the dining room and accesses the screened porch. The rear screened porch is vaulted and provides space for brisk entertaining at seasonal times of the year. Two family bedrooms share a full hall bath and the master bedroom contains an exclusive bath with a large walk-in closet. The utility room and the garage with a workbench complete the first floor.

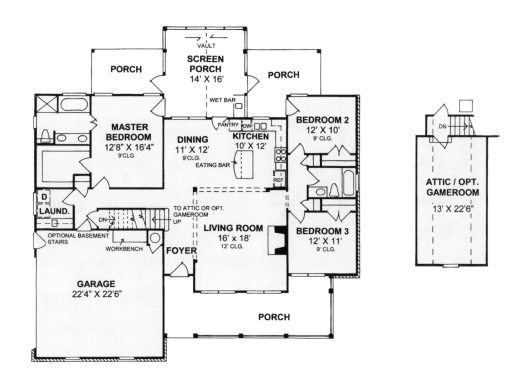

Homes for America's heartland

DESIGN HPT740084

TOTAL: 2,860 square feet

FIRST FLOOR: 2,070 square feet

SECOND FLOOR: 790 square feet

BEDROOMS: 4

BATHROOMS: 3½

WIDTH: 57'-6" **DEPTH:** 54'-0"

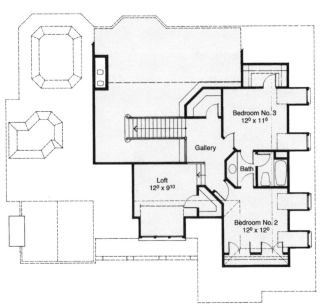

WOOD SHINGLES add a cozy touch to the exterior of this home. Interior rooms include the great room with a bay window and a fireplace, the formal dining room, and the study with another fireplace. A guest room on the first floor contains a full bath and walk-in closet. The relaxing master suite is also on the first floor and features a pampering master bath with His and Hers walk-in closets, dual vanities, a separate shower and a whirlpool tub. The second floor holds two additional bedrooms, a loft area and a gallery which overlooks the central hall. This home is designed with a walkout basement foundation.

DESIGN HPT740085

SQUARE FOOTAGE: 2,787

BONUS SPACE: 636 square feet

BEDROOMS: 4

BATHROOMS: 2½

WIDTH: 101'-0" DEPTH: 58'-8"

A LARGE COVERED PORCH in front and an angled covered veranda out back bring the outdoors into this four-bedroom Victorian design. The traffic flow throughout the main living area is perfect for entertaining large groups—the living room, dining room and study are placed conveniently near each other. The kitchen easily serves these rooms as well as the less-formal family room and breakfast nook. Upstairs, a loft and a bonus room separated by a half-wall provide room to grow. A separate shop is adjacent to the three-car garage.

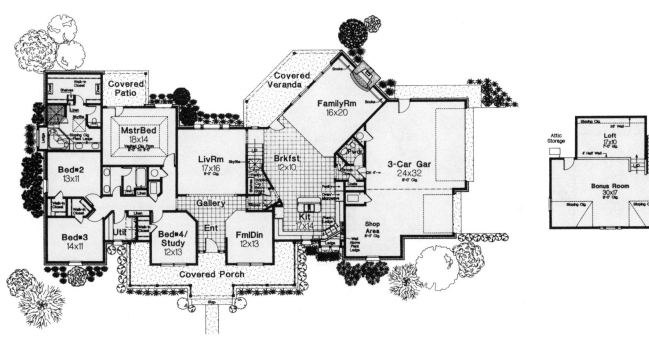

DESIGN HPT740086

SQUARE FOOTAGE: 2,293

BONUS SPACE: 536 square feet

BEDROOMS: 4

BATHROOMS: 3

WIDTH: 88'-0" DEPTH: 51'-9"

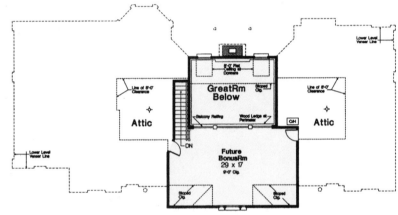

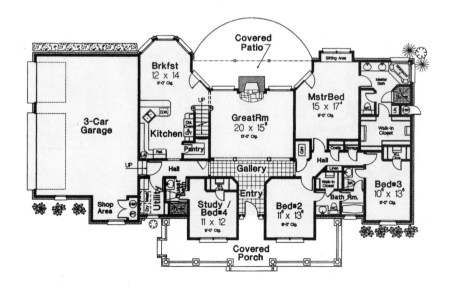

SPECIAL GATHERINGS and events will take place in the heart of this splendid home. The great room, defined by columns, includes a hearth and views to the covered patio. The east wing is occupied by the sleeping quarters with a master bedroom which features an exclusive master bath. Two family bedrooms share a compartmented bath, each with their own vanities and walk-in closets. The three-car garage opens to the hall where the utility room, the kitchen and an additional bedroom/study can be accessed. A future bonus room is also available upstairs.

DESIGN HPT740087

TOTAL: 1,920 square feet

FIRST FLOOR: 1,082 square feet

SECOND FLOOR: 838 square feet

BEDROOMS: 3

BATHROOMS: 2½

WIDTH: 66'-10" **DEPTH:** 29'-5"

FARMHOUSE FRESH WITH A TOUCH of Victorian style best describes this charming home. A covered front porch wraps around the dining room's bay window and leads the way to the entrance. To the right of the entry is a living room that features a wet bar and a warming fireplace. At the rear of the plan, an L-shaped kitchen is equipped with an island cooktop, making meal preparation a breeze. Casual meals can be enjoyed in a dining area which merges with the kitchen and accesses the rear patio. A powder room and utility room complete the first floor. Sleeping quarters contained on the second floor include a relaxing master suite with a large walk-in closet, two family bedrooms and a connecting bath.

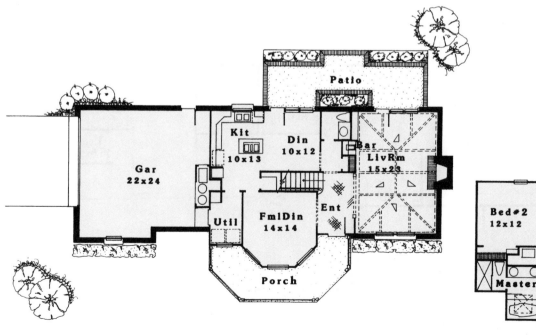

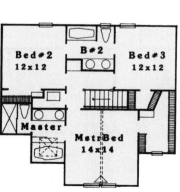

DESIGN HPT740088

SQUARE FOOTAGE: 1,688

BEDROOMS: 3

BATHROOMS: 2

WIDTH: 70'-1" DEPTH: 48'-0"

DORMERS AND COLUMNS DECORATE the exterior of this three-bedroom country home. Inside, the foyer immediately accesses one family bedroom and the formal dining area. Ahead is the great room with a warming fireplace and ribbon windows for natural lighting. The galley kitchen adjoins a breakfast area with a lovely bay window. The master suite to the back of the plan features a lavish bath with a garden tub, separate shower and two vanities. Storage is not a problem in this comfortable home, with walk-in closets in each bedroom and an additional storage room off the two-car garage. Please specify basement, crawlspace or slab foundation when ordering.

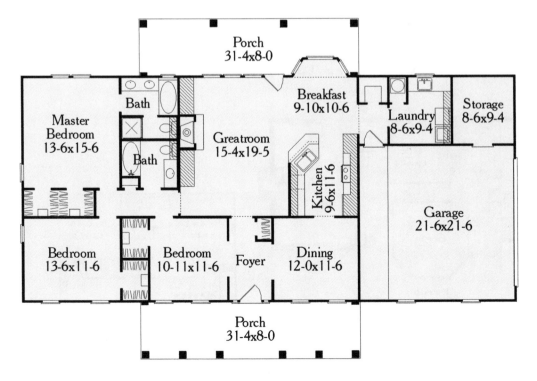

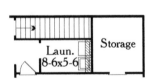

DESIGN HPT740089

TOTAL: 5,084 square feet

FIRST FLOOR: 3,170 square feet

SECOND FLOOR: 1,914 square feet

BONUS SPACE: 445 square feet

BEDROOMS: 4

BATHROOMS: 3½

WIDTH: 100'-10" **DEPTH:** 65'-5"

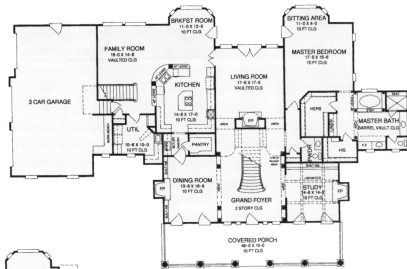

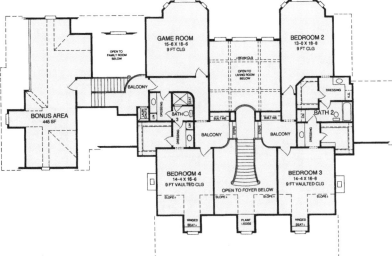

REMINISCENT OF THE GRAND homes of the Old South, this elegantly appointed home is a beauty inside and out. A centerpiece stair rises gracefully from the two-story grand foyer and features balcony overlooks to the foyer and living room. The kitchen, breakfast room and family room provide open space for the gathering of family and friends. The beam-ceilinged study and the dining room flank the grand foyer and each includes a fireplace. The master bedroom features a cozy sitting area and a luxury master bath with His and Hers vanities and walk-in closets. Three large bedrooms and a game room complete the second floor. A large expandable area is available at the top of the rear stair.

Homes for America's heartland

DESIGN HPT740090

TOTAL: 4,298 square feet

FIRST FLOOR: 2,945 square feet

SECOND FLOOR: 1,353 square feet

FINISHED BASEMENT: 1,293 square feet

BEDROOMS: 5

BATHROOMS: 5½ +½

WIDTH: 61'-4" **DEPTH:** 72'-2"

TAKE ADVANTAGE OF THE VIEWS from the second-story porch of this grand home. Inside, this home considers each household member's needs with private baths in all three family bedrooms. The master bedroom boasts His and Hers closets, a whirlpool tub, separate shower and double sinks. Near the family room—with a fireplace— the U-shaped kitchen features a twelve-inch bar top and an island accessing the nearby dining room. Guests have the option of utilizing stairs or an elevator. The basement is designed with a fifth bedroom, recreational, mechanical and storage rooms. A two-car garage protects vehicles from the weather.

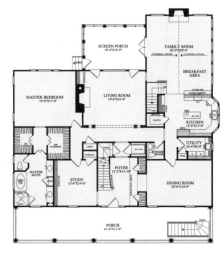

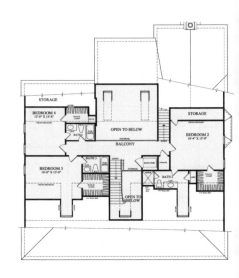

DESIGN HPT740091

TOTAL: 2,071 square feet

MAIN LEVEL: 1,376 square feet

UPPER LEVEL: 695 square feet

OPTIONAL LOWER LEVEL: 723 square feet

BEDROOMS: 4

BATHROOMS: 3½

WIDTH: 47'-0" DEPTH: 49'-8"

BEHIND THIS ATTRACTIVE facade resides a comfortable floor plan and room for the entire family. On the west wing, the kitchen is placed between the breakfast area and the dining room—a pantry is nearby. Just off the great room is the master bedroom that features its own private bath with a walk-in closet. Access to the screened porch is available on the main level—on the upper level there is an open balcony, two family bedrooms and a full hall bath. The optional level can provide a two-car garage, an additional bedroom, a full hall bath and a recreation room.

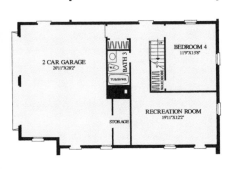

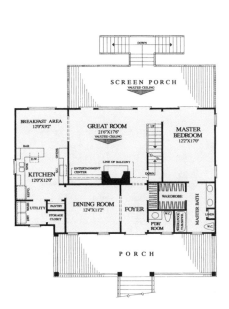

DESIGN HPT740092

TOTAL: 2,309 square feet

MAIN LEVEL: 1,554 square feet

UPPER LEVEL: 755 square feet

OPTIONAL LOWER LEVEL: 869 square feet

BEDROOMS: 4

BATHROOMS: 3½

WIDTH: 57'-6" DEPTH: 39'-6"

THERE IS NO BETTER PLACE than a private covered porch or a deck to soak up the morning sun. This two-story home provides just that and a livable floor plan. On the upper level are two family bedrooms with private access to a full bath with a compartmented shower and toilet. The main level provides the comfort of a large great room with a fireplace and a dining room united with a breakfast area by the pass-through kitchen. In the master bedroom, a full bath with double-bowl sinks, a whirlpool tub and a separate shower are available for stress-free mornings.

DESIGN HPT740093

TOTAL: 4,227 square feet

FIRST FLOOR: 2,891 square feet

SECOND FLOOR: 1,336 square feet

RECREATION ROOM: 380 square feet

BEDROOMS: 4

BATHROOMS: 3½ +½

WIDTH: 90'-8" DEPTH: 56'-4"

STUDY IN THE PRIVACY of your home in a luxurious master suite library or enjoy the sunset on the covered porch. The luxuries continue to appear throughout this graceful home. In the utility room a sink and a folding counter make laundry days a cinch. An elite master bath with a whirlpool tub and a private linen closet is provided in the master bedroom. The breakfast area is connected to the island kitchen by a bar and leads to the study area and rear porch. Bedrooms 3 and 4 share a private bath upstairs. Bedroom 2 is around the corner from the recreation room and the study loft, complete with a computer work station. Storage is also available on the second floor.

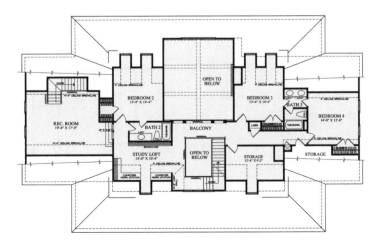

DESIGN HPT740094

SQUARE FOOTAGE: 2,465
BEDROOMS: 4
BATHROOMS: 2½
WIDTH: 65'-1" DEPTH: 64'-2"

THIS HOME BOASTS a well-laid-out design that promotes comfort and flow. The great room offers two sets of French doors to the rear porch, a fireplace, and a spacious layout perfect for entertaining. The open island kitchen shares an area with the breakfast room and connects to the dining room. The master suite delights in a room-sized sitting area, His and Hers walk-in closets and vanities, a compartmented toilet, and a separate tub and shower. Please specify basement, crawlspace or slab foundation when ordering.

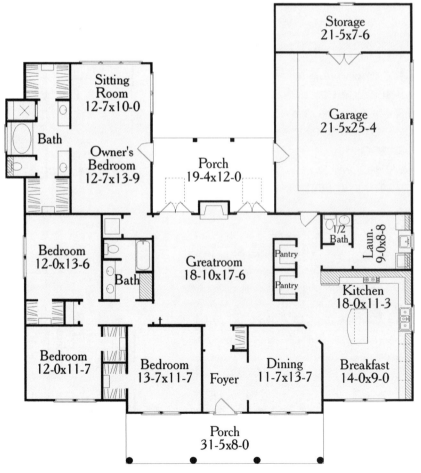

Storage
21-5x7-6

Garage
21-5x25-4

Sitting Room
12-7x10-0

Bath

Owner's Bedroom
12-7x13-9

Porch
19-4x12-0

1/2 Bath

Laun.
9-0x8-8

Bedroom
12-0x13-6

Bath

Greatroom
18-10x17-6

Pantry

Pantry

Kitchen
18-0x11-3

Bedroom
12-0x11-7

Bedroom
13-7x11-7

Foyer

Dining
11-7x13-7

Breakfast
14-0x9-0

Porch
31-5x8-0

DESIGN HPT740095

SQUARE FOOTAGE: 1,692

BONUS SPACE: 358 square feet

BEDROOMS: 3

BATHROOMS: 2

WIDTH: 54'-0" DEPTH: 56'-6"

THIS COZY COUNTRY cottage is enhanced with a front-facing planter box above the garage and a charming covered porch. The foyer leads to a vaulted great room, complete with a fireplace and radius windows. Decorative columns complement the entrance to the dining room, as does a decorative arch. On the left side of the plan resides the master suite, which is resplendent with amenities including a vaulted sitting room, tray ceiling, French doors to the vaulted full bath and an arched opening to the sitting room. On the right side, two additional bedrooms share a full bath. Please specify basement or crawlspace foundation when ordering.

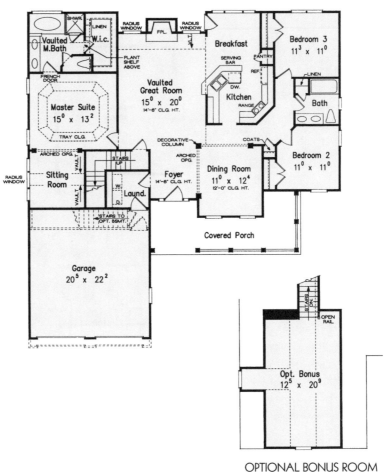

OPTIONAL BONUS ROOM

DESIGN HPT740096

TOTAL: 2,255 square feet

FIRST FLOOR: 2,159 square feet

UPPER LIBRARY: 96 square feet

FUTURE SPACE: 878 square feet

BEDROOMS: 3

BATHROOMS: 2

WIDTH: 59'-0" DEPTH: 86'-0"

THIS PLAN CHARMS instantly with its muntin windows, decorative French-style shutters, stucco exterior and steeply sloping roof complete with dormers. A large living room accesses the rear porch. The kitchen is replete with luxuries: a desk, butler's pantry and plenty of counter space. An adjacent eating area boasts bay windows and looks out to the rear property. On the right side of the plan, two bedrooms share a full bath and feature private walk-in closets. On the left side, a luxurious master suite is complete with double walk-in closets, His and Hers sinks, a garden tub and a separate shower. Please specify basement, crawlspace or slab foundation when ordering.

DESIGN HPT740097

SQUARE FOOTAGE: 2,046

BEDROOMS: 3

BATHROOMS: 2½

WIDTH: 68'-2" DEPTH: 57'-4"

A SIX-PANEL DOOR with an arched transom makes an impressive entry. Upon entering the foyer, the formal dining room resides to the right. The great room comes complete with a cozy fireplace and built-ins. On the far left of the home, two bedrooms share a full bath and a linen closet. The kitchen and breakfast room provide an ample amount of space for the family to enjoy meals together. The rear porch is also accessible from a rear bedroom and from an angled door between the great room and breakfast room. In the master bedroom, two walk-in closets provide plenty of space and two separate vanities make dressing less crowded. Please specify basement, crawlspace or slab foundation when ordering.

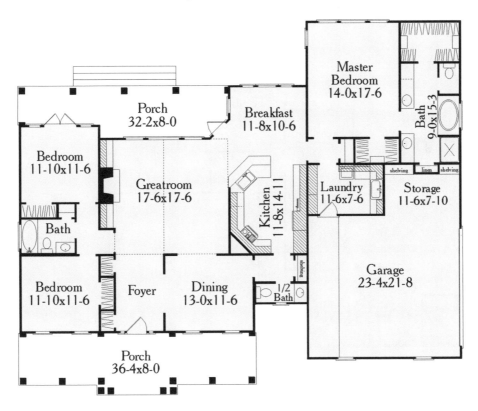

DESIGN HPT740098

SQUARE FOOTAGE: 1,698

BEDROOMS: 3

BATHROOMS: 2

WIDTH: 66'-0" DEPTH: 49'-11"

GABLES, COLUMNS AND MULTI-PANE WINDOWS give this ranch-style home great curb appeal. A columned foyer branches off into the great room, formal dining area and two family bedrooms. A fireplace warms the great room and is visible from the kitchen. The adjoining kitchen and breakfast area enjoy an island/snack bar and a ribbon of windows facing the rear yard. The master suite is privately tucked behind the kitchen and accesses the rear porch. Please specify basement, crawlspace or slab foundation when ordering.

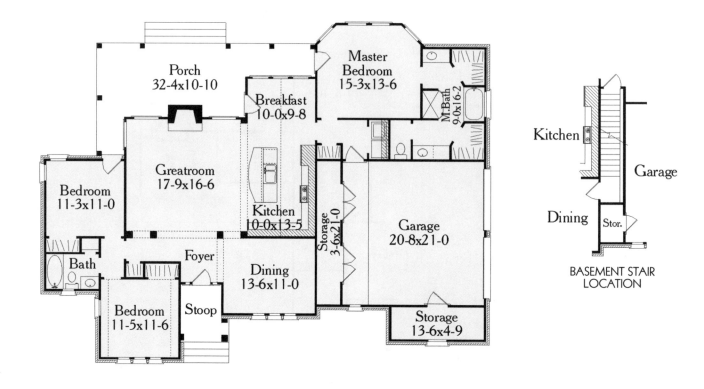

DESIGN HPT740099

SQUARE FOOTAGE: 2,053

BEDROOMS: 3

BATHROOMS: 2

WIDTH: 57'-8" **DEPTH:** 71'-10"

SHUTTERS, MULTI-PANE glass windows and a cross-hatched railing on the front porch make this a beautiful country cottage. To the left of the foyer is a roomy great room and a warming fireplace, framed by windows. To the right of the foyer, two family bedrooms feature walk-in closets and share a fully appointed bath. The efficient kitchen centers around a long island workstation and opens to the large dining/sitting room. The rear porch adds living space to view the outdoors. French doors, a fireplace and columns complete this three-bedroom design. Please specify basement, crawlspace or slab foundation when ordering.

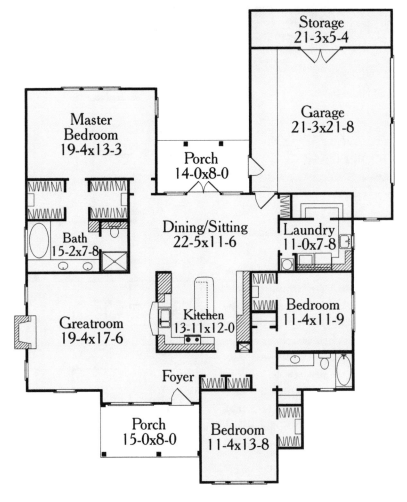

DESIGN HPT740100

SQUARE FOOTAGE: 2,555

BEDROOMS: 4

BATHROOMS: 2½

WIDTH: 66'-1" **DEPTH:** 77'-7"

A STEEPLY PITCHED ROOF and transoms over multi-pane windows give this house great curb appeal. To the left of the foyer is the formal dining room with through access to the kitchen and breakfast area. A large island/snack bar adds plenty of counter space for food preparation. Double French doors frame the fireplace in the great room, leading to the skylit covered porch at the rear of the home. The master suite has a light-filled sitting room and luxurious bath with two walk-in closets, a garden tub and separate shower. Please specify basement, crawlspace or slab foundation when ordering.

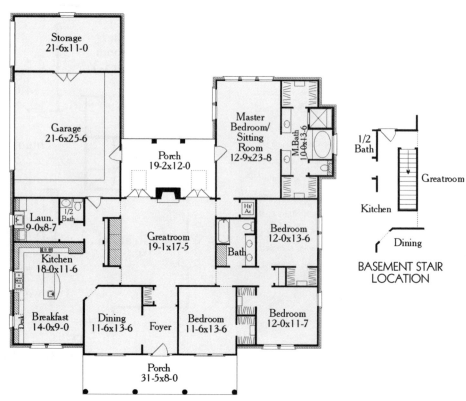

Storage
21-6x11-0

Garage
21-6x25-6

Porch
19-2x12-0

Master
Bedroom/
Sitting
Room
12-9x23-8

M.Bath
10-0x13-6

1/2
Bath

Greatroom

Kitchen

Dining

BASEMENT STAIR
LOCATION

Laun.
9-0x8-7

1/2
Bath

Greatroom
19-1x17-5

Bath

Bedroom
12-0x13-6

Kitchen
18-0x11-6

Breakfast
14-0x9-0

Dining
11-6x13-6

Foyer

Bedroom
11-6x13-6

Bedroom
12-0x11-7

Porch
31-5x8-0

DESIGN HPT740101

SQUARE FOOTAGE: 2,506

BEDROOMS: 4

BATHROOMS: 2½

WIDTH: 72'-2" DEPTH: 66'-4"

A PORCH FULL of columns gives a relaxing emphasis to this country home. To the right of the foyer, the dining area resides conveniently near the efficient kitchen. The kitchen island, walk-in pantry and serving bar add plenty of work space to the food-preparation zone. Natural light fills the breakfast nook through a ribbon of windows. Escape to the relaxing master suite featuring a private sun room/retreat and a luxurious bath set between His and Hers walk-in closets. The great room features a warming fireplace and built-ins. Please specify basement, crawlspace or slab foundation when ordering.

Master Bedroom

Laundry
6-6x7-0

1/2 Bath

Storage

BASEMENT STAIR
LOCATION

Retreat
15-4x8-0

M.Bath
12-3x11-10

Master Bedroom
15-4x15-8

Porch
20-4x8-0

Breakfast
10-0x13-0

Pantry

Laundry
11-2x7-0

Bedroom
11-9x13-6

Bath

Greatroom
15-9x17-6

Kitchen
12-6x12-3

1/2 Bath

Storage
11-2x3-9

Garage
21-8x21-8

Bedroom
11-6x11-6

Bedroom
11-6x11-6

Foyer

Dining
13-5x11-6

Porch
33-9x8-0

DESIGN HPT740102

SQUARE FOOTAGE: 2,267

BEDROOMS: 4

BATHROOMS: 2½

WIDTH: 71'-2" DEPTH: 62'-0"

SIX COLUMNS and a steeply pitched roof lend elegance to this four-bedroom home. To the right of the foyer, the dining area sits conveniently near the efficient island kitchen that enjoys plenty of work space. Natural light will flood the breakfast nook through a ribbon of windows facing the rear yard. Escape to the relaxing master bedroom, with its luxurious bath set between His and Hers walk-in closets. The great room is complete with a warming fireplace and built-ins. Three family bedrooms enjoy private walk-in closets and share a fully appointed bath. Please specify basement, crawlspace or slab foundation when ordering.

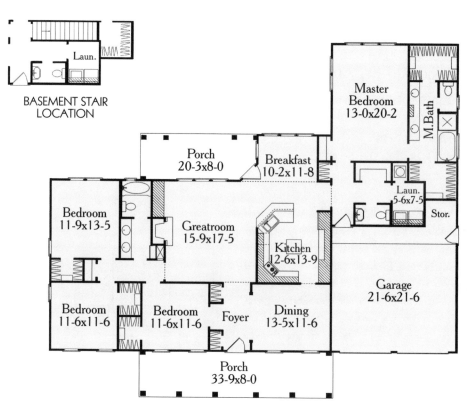

BASEMENT STAIR
LOCATION

Laun.

Porch
20-3x8-0

Breakfast
10-2x11-8

Master
Bedroom
13-0x20-2

M. Bath

Bedroom
11-9x13-5

Greatroom
15-9x17-5

Kitchen
12-6x13-9

Laun.
5-6x7-5

Stor.

Bedroom
11-6x11-6

Bedroom
11-6x11-6

Foyer

Dining
13-5x11-6

Garage
21-6x21-6

Porch
33-9x8-0

DESIGN HPT740103

SQUARE FOOTAGE: 1,997

BEDROOMS: 4

BATHROOMS: 2½

WIDTH: 56'-4" DEPTH: 67'-4"

THE WIDE FRONT STEPS, columned porch and symmetrical layout give this charming home a Georgian appeal. The central great room offers radiant French doors on both sides of the fireplace. Outside those doors is a comfortable covered porch with two skylights, expanding the livable space to the outdoors. The large kitchen with its walk-in pantry, island/snack bar and breakfast nook will gratify any cook. To the left of the great room reside four bedrooms—three secondary bedrooms and a master suite. The master suite enjoys a walk-in closet, twin vanity sinks, a separate shower and tub, and private access to the rear porch. Please specify basement, crawlspace or slab foundation when ordering.

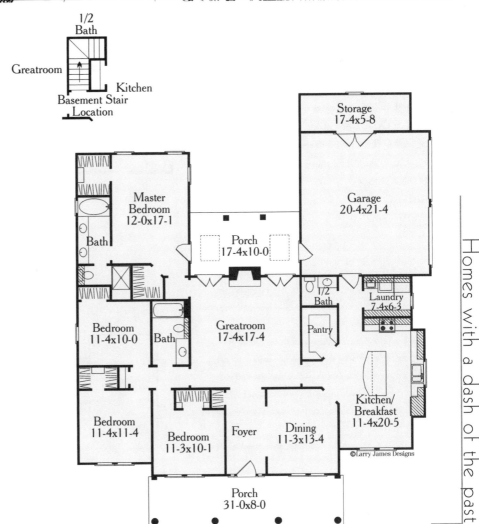

Homes with a dash of the past

DESIGN HPT740104

TOTAL: 3,002 square feet

FIRST FLOOR: 1,904 square feet

SECOND FLOOR: 1,098 square feet

FUTURE SPACE: 522 square feet

BEDROOMS: 4

BATHROOMS: 4½

WIDTH: 88'-2" DEPTH: 54'-0"

THIS UNIQUE EXTERIOR design presents an open yet cozy floor plan. A built-in entertainment center and a cathedral ceiling create a spacious area that leads to the breakfast area and island kitchen. The dining area and the terrace are both accessible from the breakfast area. Privacy is allowed in the master bedroom placed to far right of the design—it's complemented with a master bath built for two and a walk-in closet with a window seat. At the top of the stairs is a balcony and a hall leading to a future recreation room. Three bedrooms, each with full baths, are also available on the second floor.

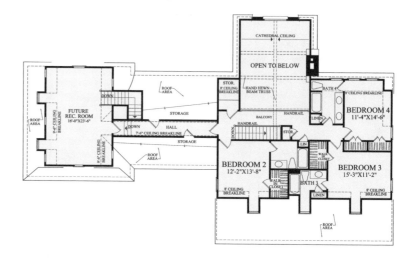

DESIGN HPT740105

TOTAL: 2,276 square feet

FIRST FLOOR: 1,664 square feet

SECOND FLOOR: 612 square feet

BEDROOMS: 3

BATHROOMS: 2½

WIDTH: 66'-0" DEPTH: 39'-0"

A CALMING SYMMETRY infuses this wonderful three-bedroom country home. Pillars adorn the exterior and interior of the plan. A balcony overlooks the entry of all guests to the foyer. The hearth-warmed living room opens to the left of the foyer. Just around the corner, the sun-filled dining room features a cathedral ceiling and French doors that access the rear deck. The roomy kitchen also enjoys French-door access to the rear deck and includes a large island snack bar and a pantry. The master suite is a wonderful retreat with a sunny sitting room and private porch. Two family bedrooms share a full bath on the second level. Please specify basement or crawlspace foundation when ordering.

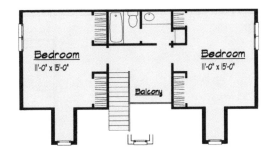

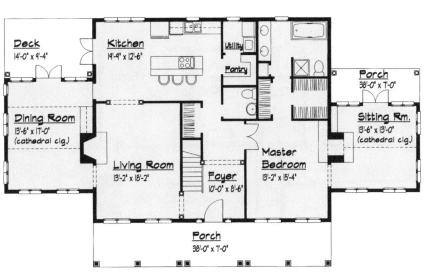

DESIGN HPT740106

TOTAL: 1,513 square feet

FIRST FLOOR: 790 square feet

SECOND FLOOR: 723 square feet

BONUS SPACE: 285 square feet

BEDROOMS: 3

BATHROOMS: 2½

WIDTH: 49'-8" DEPTH: 30'-6"

Bedroom 10'8" x 10'4"

Bedroom 10'9" x 10'8"

walk-in closet

Bonus Room 17'9" x 11'

Hall

Bath

Bath

stairs dn

Master, Bedroom 12' x 16'

plant shelf

walk-in closet

slope ceiling

slope ceiling

Laun.

Kitchen 10'4" x 13'4"

Dining Room 12' x 12'8"

pantry

Two-car Garage 19' x 20'

Great Room 20' x 14'6"

Porch

THE NOSTALGIA OF a more relaxed time, when neighbors visited and shared evening conversation, is provided with the exterior style of this delightful home. Large rooms and a clean, easy floor plan offer value and efficiency. Upgraded features include a first-floor utility room, a two-car garage, counter space with seating availability, a pantry and a fireplace. The spacious second floor boasts a generous-sized master bedroom including a private bath and roomy walk-in closet. Two additional bedrooms and a large bonus room that can be finished later complete this comfortable home.

DESIGN HPT740107

SQUARE FOOTAGE: 1,694

BONUS SPACE: 115 square feet

BEDROOMS: 3

BATHROOMS: 2½

WIDTH: 38'-0" DEPTH: 63'-3"

THIS 1½ STORY HOME fits effortlessly in either the wooded countryside or a manicured suburb. A multitude of well-placed windows floods the interior with fresh air and sunlight. The great room, with its warming fireplace, is open to the formal dining room where sliding glass doors open to the expansive backyard deck. The lavish master suite on the first floor offers privacy and a luxurious bath. Two additional bedrooms share a full bath on the second floor. Please specify crawlspace or basement foundation when ordering.

Deck
14'-4" x 22'-4"

Garage
20'-0" x 20'-0"

Storage
14'-0" x 4'-0"

Kitchen
10'-0" x 14'-5"

Utility

Dining Rm.
10'-0" x 14'-5"

Pantry

Great Room
20'-0" x 16'-3"
(cathedral clg.)

Master Bedroom
13'-5" x 16'-3"

Porch
22'-8" x 6'-8"

Bedroom
14'-2" x 11'-10"

Bedroom
13'-5" x 11'-10"

Balcony

open to Great Room below

Bonus Rm.
13'-5" x 7'-2"

THIS HOME IS PACKED with all-American charm and no small number of features. On either side of the large entry foyer are a formal dining room and a living room with a gigantic bay window, a fireplace and access to a covered porch overlooking the backyard. Dominating the back of the first floor is an enormous country kitchen. The efficient U-shaped work area here is complemented by a number of amenities: an exposed-beam ceiling, a raised-hearth fireplace, a bay window and built-in shelves. A washroom and a laundry are close by. The cozy second floor holds three bedrooms and two full baths. Cleverly designed window seats in the dormer windows hide small storage areas.

DESIGN HPT740108

TOTAL: 2,085 square feet
FIRST FLOOR: 1,217 square feet
SECOND FLOOR: 868 square feet
BEDROOMS: 3
BATHROOMS: 2½
WIDTH: 49'-8" DEPTH: 44'-0"

L

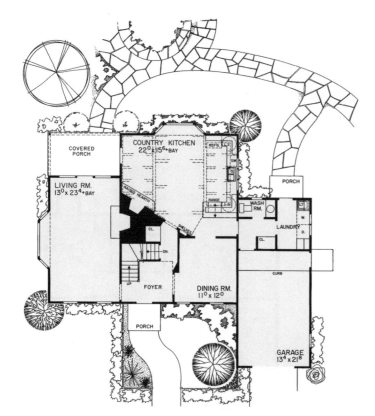

QUOTE ONE®
Cost to build? See page 214
to order complete cost estimate
to build this house in your area!

DESIGN HPT740109

SQUARE FOOTAGE: 2,170

BEDROOMS: 3

BATHROOMS: 2½

WIDTH: 63'-6" DEPTH: 61'-0"

THE COVERED FRONT PORCH leads to a foyer flanked by formal living and dining rooms. The spacious family room opens to the breakfast bay. The well-positioned kitchen, with an island, easily serves the formal and informal areas. The master suite has a tray ceiling in the sleeping area and a vaulted ceiling in the bath. The two other bedrooms flank a full bath with a double-bowl vanity. A two-car garage offers optional basement stairs.

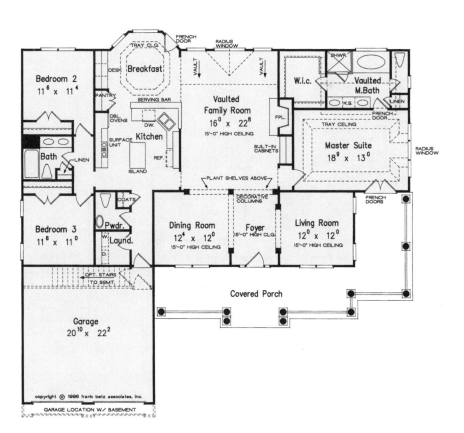

Homes with a dash of the past

DESIGN HPT740110

TOTAL: 2,253 square feet

FIRST FLOOR: 1,634 square feet

SECOND FLOOR: 619 square feet

FUTURE SPACE: 229 square feet

BEDROOMS: 3

BATHROOMS: 2½

WIDTH: 46'-0" DEPTH: 54'-5"

THE EXTERIOR OF this adorable home is flattered with shutters, muntin windows and columns defining the front porch. Inside, this home features a central family room and island kitchen with a breakfast area and a dinning room. Across from the utility room is a powder room and a nearby living room. The master bedroom resides on the first floor while two bedrooms and a full hall bath are located on the second floor. A future recreation room is optional above the two-car garage.

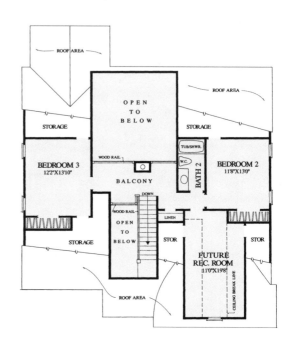

DESIGN HPT740111

TOTAL: 2,792 square feet

FIRST FLOOR: 2,015 square feet

SECOND FLOOR: 777 square feet

BEDROOMS: 3

BATHROOMS: 2½

WIDTH: 58'-4" **DEPTH:** 59'-10"

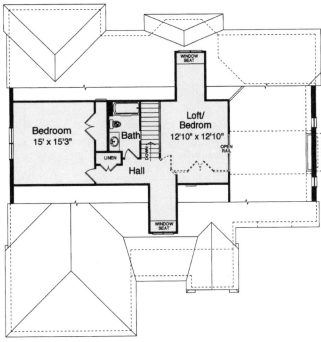

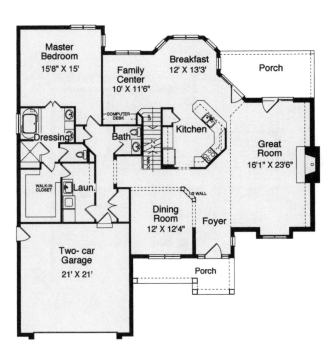

A COVERED PORCH, boxed window and dormer decorate the exterior of this delightfully designed home. At the foyer, an impressive view is offered to the formal dining room and through to the large great room. The great room lives up to its name with a high ceiling, fireplace and French doors that expand the living space to a covered porch. Angled walls wrap around the breakfast room and a counter with seating at the kitchen—adding a delightful transition between the great room and breakfast room. A cozy area adjoining the breakfast room could provide a flexible family center with a built-in desk. The master bedroom suite offers luxury to the homeowners and access to the laundry room from the closet. Rear stairs lead to a second-floor bedroom and loft, providing a dramatic view to the great room.

Homes with a dash of the past

DESIGN HPT740112

TOTAL: 2,640 square feet

FIRST FLOOR: 1,810 square feet

SECOND FLOOR: 830 square feet

BEDROOMS: 4

BATHROOMS: 3½

WIDTH: 68'-0" DEPTH: 54'-0"

SUNBURST WINDOWS and a covered veranda work together to allow just enough sunlight into the great room and the family room. The entry way, which also features a sunburst window, leads to the U-shaped kitchen with a breakfast room accessible to the covered patio. A second entrance to the covered patio exists in the master bedroom—which is accompanied by an extensive master bath. Upstairs are three family bedrooms, Bedroom 4 includes a full private bath and may serve as a playroom.

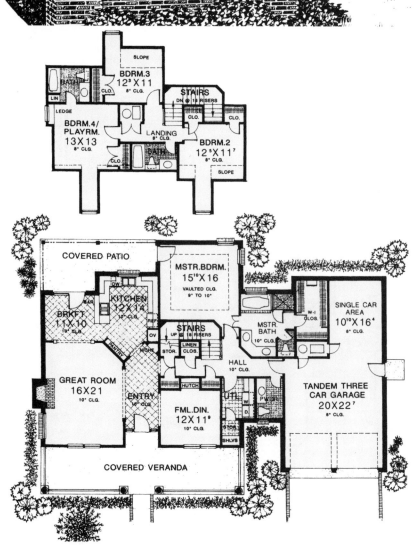

DESIGN HPT740113

TOTAL: 1,349 square feet

FIRST FLOOR: 778 square feet

SECOND FLOOR: 571 square feet

BEDROOMS: 3

BATHROOMS: 2½

WIDTH: 38'-0" **DEPTH:** 45'-6"

DOUBLE COLUMNS ALONG with transoms and a sunburst create an enticing entrance. The living room with a fireplace is accessible to the island kitchen. Double doors in the kitchen lead to the covered porch in the backyard. The utility room and pantry are strategically placed near the powder room. The master suite is sumptuous; it includes its own fireplace and a private bath with dual vanities. Two family bedrooms can be found upstairs, both with two closets. A full hall bath is also provided on the second floor. Please specify basement or crawlspace foundation when ordering.

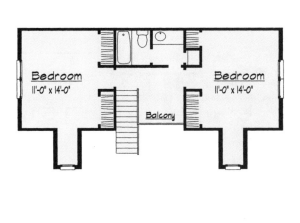

Homes with a dash of the past

TWIN CHIMNEYS, A WIDOW'S WALK, prominent dormers and a five-sided porch enhance the gracious exterior of this historical adaptation. The entry foyer features a grand staircase and opens onto formal areas with a generous living room to the left, and a banquet-sized dining room to the right. An island kitchen located at the rear of the plan includes a large walk-in pantry and an adjacent morning room. The spacious family room located nearby enjoys a raised-hearth fireplace and a wraparound porch. Rear stairs serve the future living area above the three-car garage and also access the lower-level guest room and recreation room. The second floor contains a huge master suite, which includes a small kitchenette. Two family bedrooms—each with walk-in closets and separate dressing areas--share a full bath.

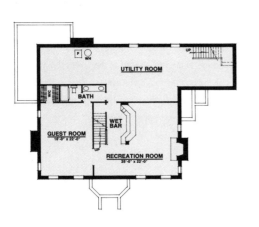

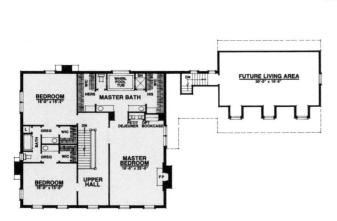

DESIGN HPT740114

TOTAL: 3,684 square feet

FIRST FLOOR: 1,997 square feet

SECOND FLOOR: 1,687 square feet

BONUS SPACE: 582 square feet

FINISHED BASEMENT 960 square feet

BEDROOMS: 3

BATHROOMS: 2½ +½

WIDTH: 96'-0" DEPTH: 54'-8"

DESIGN HPT740115

TOTAL: 4,594 square feet

FIRST FLOOR: 3,294 square feet

SECOND FLOOR: 1,300 square feet

BEDROOMS: 5

BATHROOMS: 3½

WIDTH: 106'-10" **DEPTH:** 52'-10"

THE CHARM OF THE OLD SOUTH is designed into this stately Federal manor. A round entry portico leads to the two-story foyer with a circular staircase. The formal living room, dining room and family room each feature a distinctive fireplace; the latter is also highlighted by a built-in entertainment center, walk-in wet bar, beamed cathedral ceiling, and access to a rear covered patio. Impressive ten-foot ceilings grace the entire first floor. The secluded master bedroom has a vaulted ceiling, three walk-in closets and patio access. Four additional bedrooms on the second floor share adjoining baths.

Homes with a dash of the past

DESIGN HPT740116

TOTAL: 3,445 square feet

FIRST FLOOR: 1,666 square feet

SECOND FLOOR: 1,779 square feet

BEDROOMS: 4

BATHROOMS: 3½

WIDTH: 71'-8" **DEPTH:** 38'-10"

Bedroom
13'7" x 17'1"
8' ceiling height

Dressing

laundry chute

walk-in closet

computer desk

Dressing

Master Bedroom
16'11" x 20'8"
9' ceiling height

Hall

linen

Bedroom
16'10" x 12'9"
8' ceiling height

stairs dn
4 risers

walk-in closet

Bath

walk-in closet

stairs dn

wood rail

Balcony

Bedroom
15'10" x 12'0"
9' ceiling height

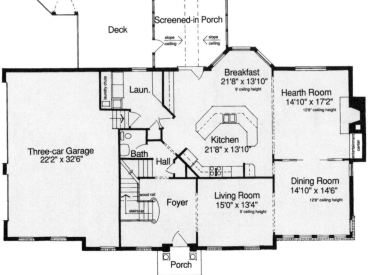

Gazebo

Deck

Screened-in Porch

slope ceiling

slope ceiling

Breakfast
21'8" x 13'10"
9' ceiling height

Hearth Room
14'10" x 17'2"
12'8" ceiling height

Laun.

laundry chute

Kitchen
21'8" x 13'10"

entertainment center

Three-car Garage
22'2" x 32'6"

Bath

Hall

Dining Room
14'10" x 14'6"
12'8" ceiling height

wood rail

stairs up

Foyer

Living Room
15'0" x 13'4"
9' ceiling height

Porch

THIS TWO-STORY BRICK HOME is reminiscent of an Early American design. The flow of the first floor creates ease of entertaining guests in the formal living room and dining room, while a comfortable and inviting atmosphere for family enjoyment exists in the kitchen and spacious hearth room. Wood rails and newel posts decorate the stairs leading to a separate wing on the mid-level, offering children's bedrooms and a computer space. The master bedroom suite, with its sitting area, fireplace and deluxe bath/dressing room combines to create a fabulous retreat.

DESIGN HPT740117

TOTAL: 5,220 square feet
FIRST FLOOR: 3,599 square feet
SECOND FLOOR: 1,621 square feet
BONUS SPACE: 356 square feet
BEDROOMS: 4
BATHROOMS: 5½
WIDTH: 108'-10" **DEPTH:** 53'-10"

A grand facade detailed with brick corner quoins, stucco flourishes, arched windows and an elegant entrance presents this home and preludes the amenities inside. A spacious foyer is accented by curving stairs and flanked by formal living and dining rooms. For cozy times, a through-fireplace is located between a large family room and a quiet study. The master bedroom is designed to pamper, with two walk-in closets (one is absolutely huge), a two-sided fireplace sharing its heat with a bayed sitting area and the bedroom, and a lavish private bath filled with attractive amenities. Upstairs, three secondary bedrooms each have a private bath and walk-in closet. Also on this level is a spacious recreation room, perfect for a game room or children's playroom.

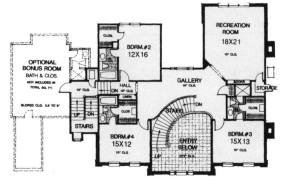

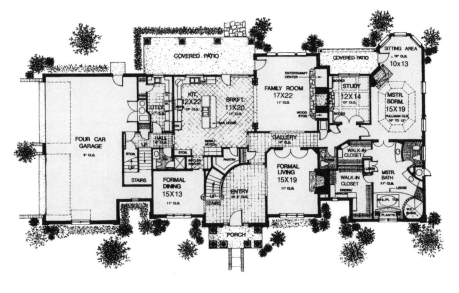

Homes with a dash of the past

DESIGN HPT740118

TOTAL: 3,335 square feet

FIRST FLOOR: 2,432 square feet

SECOND FLOOR: 903 square feet

BEDROOMS: 4

BATHROOMS: 3½

WIDTH: 90'-0" **DEPTH:** 53'-10"

THE ELEGANT SYMMETRY of this Southern traditional four-bedroom plan makes it a joy to own. Six columns frame the covered porch, and two chimneys add interest to the exterior roofline. The two-story foyer opens to the right to a formal living room with a built-in wet bar and a fireplace. A massive family room with a cathedral ceiling leads outside to a large covered patio or to the breakfast room and kitchen. A side-entry, three-car garage provides room for a golf cart and separate workshop area. The first-floor master bedroom features vaulted ceilings, a secluded covered patio and a plant ledge in the master bath.

DESIGN HPT740119

TOTAL: 2,959 square feet

FIRST FLOOR: 1,848 square feet

SECOND FLOOR: 1,111 square feet

BEDROOMS: 4

BATHROOMS: 3½

WIDTH: 73'-4" **DEPTH:** 44'-1"

EVERY HOMEOWNER'S WISH is granted with a floor plan designed to enchant family members and guests. Relish the master bedroom privileged with patio access and a divine master bath. The great room, with a hearth, is fit for casual gatherings, while the formal living and dining rooms are savored for special occasions. Outdoor relaxing and entertaining are effortless with an extended patio and a covered area. Three bedrooms, two full baths and a loft occupy the second floor. The three-car garage enters through the utility room and leads to the island kitchen.

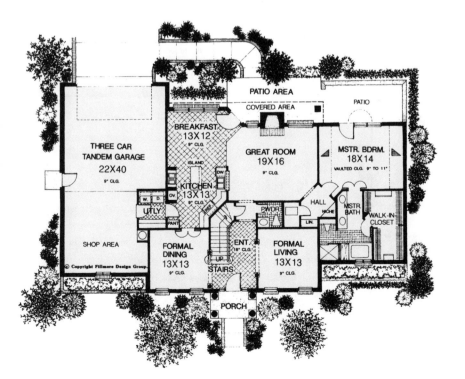

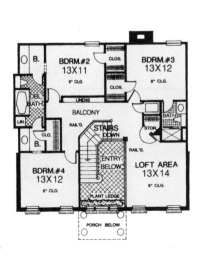

Homes with a dash of the past

DESIGN HPT740120

TOTAL: 2,106 square feet

FIRST FLOOR: 1,083 square feet

SECOND FLOOR: 1,023 square feet

FUTURE SPACE: 318 square feet

BEDROOMS: 3

BATHROOMS: 2½

WIDTH: 55'-0" DEPTH: 43'-0"

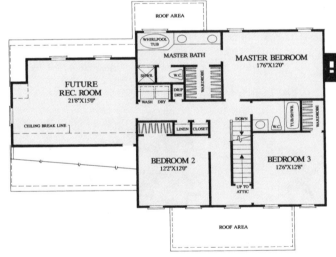

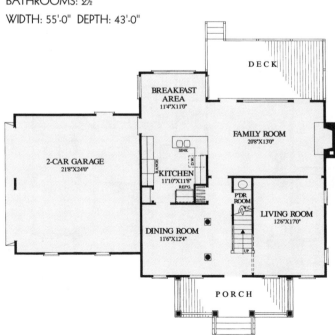

IT'S SIMPLY SUCCESS for this well-thought-out plan. The first floor is devoted to creating a livable atmosphere—with a pass-through kitchen from the breakfast area to the dining room. The family room contains a fireplace and accesses the living room and a rear deck. On the second floor, sleeping quarters are accommodated with three bedrooms, including the master bedroom with a private bath. A future recreation room may be added above the two-car garage.

DESIGN HPT740121

TOTAL: 3,553 square feet

FIRST FLOOR: 1,830 square feet

SECOND FLOOR: 1,723 square feet

FUTURE SPACE: 534 square feet

BEDROOMS: 4

BATHROOMS: 2½

WIDTH: 72'-1" DEPTH: 74'-8"

TWIN CHIMNEYS TOP THE RIDGE of this grand home, softly lit by coach lamps that flank the simple, yet elegantly framed entry. Inside, the foyer extends a cordial welcome and serves as the main traffic pattern to all areas, both formal and informal. The living room shares the warmth of a double-facing fireplace with the formal dining room. Across the hall is a study that easily serves as a library, providing a place for reflective moments or enjoying your favorite novel. Located to the side of the kitchen with its adjacent morning room is a huge family room with a warming fireplace, wraparound porch and nine-foot ceiling. All four bedrooms are found upstairs, as well as a large future living area.

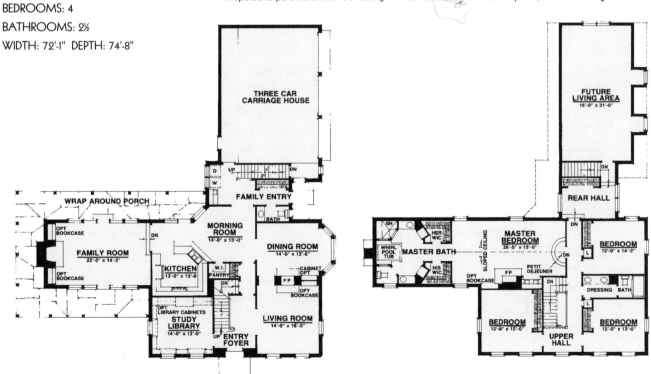

Homes with a dash of the past

DESIGN HPT740122

TOTAL: 2,450 square feet

FIRST FLOOR: 1,277 square feet

SECOND FLOOR: 1,173 square feet

BEDROOMS: 4

BATHROOMS: 3

WIDTH: 42'-0" DEPTH: 52'-10"

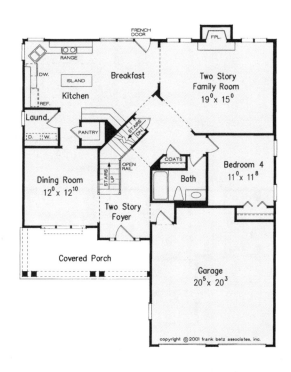

AN ARRAY OF MULTIPLE ROOFLINES and double gables set a gratifying tone to this stone and siding exterior. Under the covered porch and through the foyer is the dining room and stairs to the second floor. The two-story family room, with a hearth, is open to the breakfast area and island kitchen. French doors open the master suite that includes a vaulted bath, sitting area and tray ceiling. Two famliy bedrooms are located in the second floor and reside on the first floor near the full hall bath.

DESIGN HPT740123

TOTAL: 1,958 square feet

FIRST FLOOR: 1,074 square feet

SECOND FLOOR: 884 square feet

BONUS SPACE: 299 square feet

BEDROOMS: 3

BATHROOMS: 2½

WIDTH: 50'-10"   DEPTH: 47'-0"

THIS ATTRACTIVE HOME IS RICH WITH EXTERIOR DETAIL and offers charm coupled with modern amenities. Formal and informal spaces are provided, with the open hearth room, kitchen and breakfast area serving as an exciting gathering place for family members. The first-floor mudroom or laundry provides a buffer from the garage and outdoors. Split stairs, graced with wood banisters, lead to the second floor. The lavish master bedroom is topped with a tray ceiling and offers a deluxe bath and a large walk-in closet. A front bedroom can be converted to an open loft overlooking the stairway. Continuing to the third floor, a bonus room provides optional space and a full bath allows this to be a private bedroom retreat.

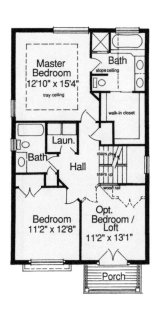

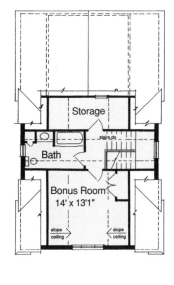

Homes with a dash of the past

DESIGN HPT740124

TOTAL: 2,151 square feet

FIRST FLOOR: 1,092 square feet

SECOND FLOOR: 1,059 square feet

BEDROOMS: 3

BATHROOMS: 2½

WIDTH: 48'-0" DEPTH: 36'-0"

VOLUME CEILINGS PLAY A PART in this design: both the family room and the foyer are two-story areas with overlooks from above. A powder room and a coat closet are directly off the foyer, which opens on the left to the living room and dining room and directly ahead to the kitchen and breakfast area. Upstairs, the master suite features a sitting room and, through French doors, a luxurious bath and walk-in closet. Two family bedrooms—one with a walk-in closet—share a bath that has a double-bowl vanity. Please specify basement or crawlspace foundation when ordering.

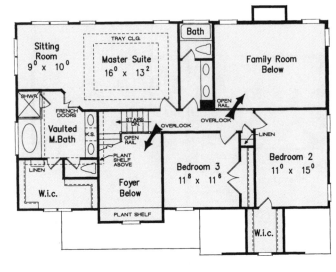

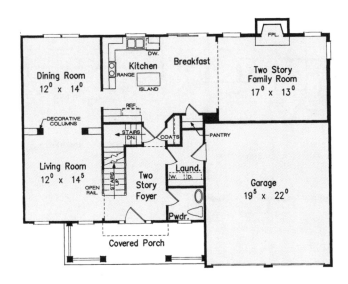

DESIGN HPT740125

TOTAL: 4,045 square feet

FIRST FLOOR: 1,999 square feet

SECOND FLOOR: 2,046 square feet

BEDROOMS: 5

BATHROOMS: 4½

WIDTH: 66'-4" DEPTH: 64'-0"

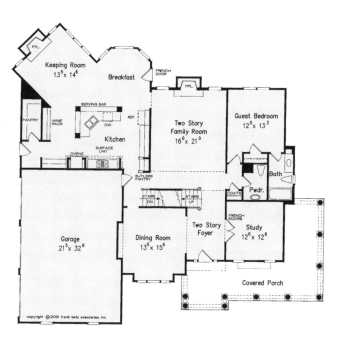

THIS LUXURY FARMHOUSE DESIGN is reserved for the hardworking homeowner who seeks a relaxing retreat. A front covered porch that wraps around the side adds a country accent to the exterior. Inside, a study and formal dining room flank the two-story foyer. A guest suite is placed to the right of the two-story family room, warmed by a fireplace. The kitchen is open to the nook and casual keeping room. A three-car garage is located nearby. Upstairs, the master suite features a hearth-warmed sitting room, private bath and two large walk-in closets. Please specify basement or crawlspace foundation when ordering.

Homes with a dash of the past

DESIGN HPT740126

TOTAL: 2,386 square feet
FIRST FLOOR: 1,223 square feet
SECOND FLOOR: 1,163 square feet
BONUS SPACE: 204 square feet
BEDROOMS: 4
BATHROOMS: 2½
WIDTH: 50'-0" **DEPTH:** 48'-0"

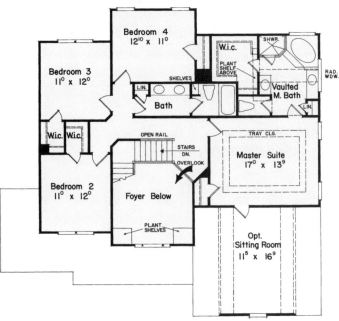

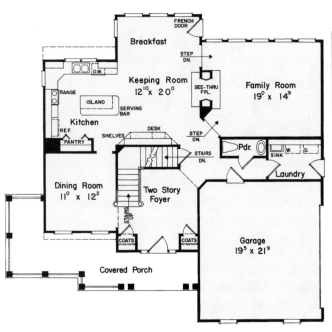

CLASSIC CAPSTONES AND ARCHED WINDOWS complement rectangular shutters and pillars on this traditional facade. The family room offsets a formal dining room and shares a see-through fireplace with the keeping room. A gourmet kitchen boasts a food-preparation island with a serving bar, a generous pantry and French-door access to the rear property. Upstairs, a sensational master suite with a tray ceiling opens from a gallery hall with a balcony overlook and features a vaulted bath with a plant shelf, whirlpool spa and walk-in closet. Bonus space offers the possibility of an adjoining sitting room. Three additional bedrooms share a full bath. Please specify basement or crawl-space foundation when ordering.

DESIGN HPT740127

TOTAL: 1,995 square feet

FIRST FLOOR: 1,071 square feet

SECOND FLOOR: 924 square feet

BONUS SPACE: 280 square feet

BEDROOMS: 3

BATHROOMS: 2½

WIDTH: 55'-10" DEPTH: 38'-6"

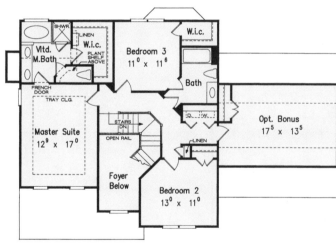

MOVE-UP BUYERS CAN ENJOY all the luxuries of this two-story home highlighted by an angled staircase separating the dining room from casual living areas. A private powder room is tucked away behind the dining room—convenient for formal dinner parties. A bay window and built-in desk in the breakfast area are just a few of the plan's amenities. The sleeping zone occupies the second floor—away from everyday activities—and includes a master suite and two secondary bedrooms. Please specify basement or crawlspace foundation when ordering.

Homes with a dash of the past

DESIGN HPT740128

TOTAL: 2,902 square feet

FIRST FLOOR: 1,438 square feet

SECOND FLOOR: 1,464 square feet

BEDROOMS: 5

BATHROOMS: 4

WIDTH: 52'-0" **DEPTH:** 64'-6"

NOTHING ON A HOME SAYS "Americana" like open pediment and covered porch detailing. Step into the two-story foyer and be formally introduced to the dining room on the left and the living room on the right. The two-story family room is a place of comfort and open space featuring a central fireplace and rear access. The kitchen and breakfast bay work well together. Five bedrooms, including a luxurious master suite, complete this plan. Please specify basement or crawlspace foundation when ordering.

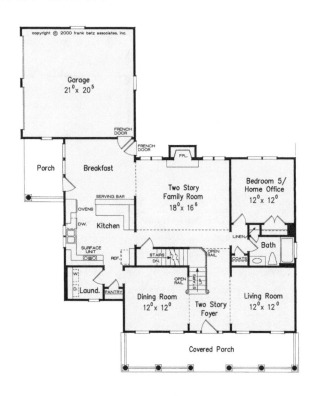

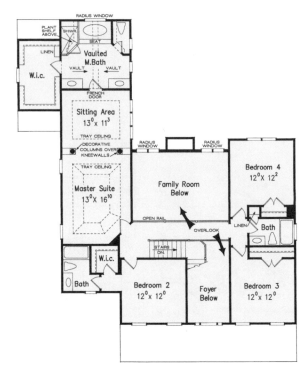

DESIGN HPT740129

TOTAL: 3,020 square feet
FIRST FLOOR: 1,887 square feet
SECOND FLOOR: 1,133 square feet
FUTURE SPACE: 444 square feet
BEDROOMS: 4
BATHROOMS: 4½
WIDTH: 63'-4" **DEPTH:** 82'-2"

ADMIRE AN EXTRAVAGANT FACADE with a two-story porch and walls of muntin windows, while inside the secluded master suite begs for occupancy. The master bath features dual-vanities, compartmented toilet, whirlpool tub and a separate shower—the extended walk-in closet allows room for double wardrobes. The bar connects the kitchen to the breakfast area with its own covered porch. Upon entering the foyer the dining room is to the left, the living room is to the right and a family room with a fireplace to straight ahead. The second floor is just as impressive with all three bedrooms displaying full private baths and walk-in closets.

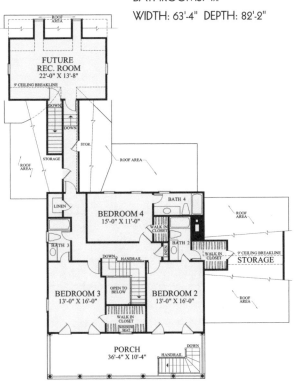

Homes with a dash of the past

137

DESIGN HPT740130

TOTAL: 3,039 square feet

FIRST FLOOR: 1,488 square feet

SECOND FLOOR: 1,551 square feet

BEDROOMS: 5

BATHROOMS: 4

WIDTH: 55'-0" DEPTH: 57'-4"

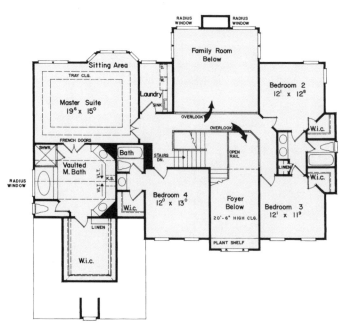

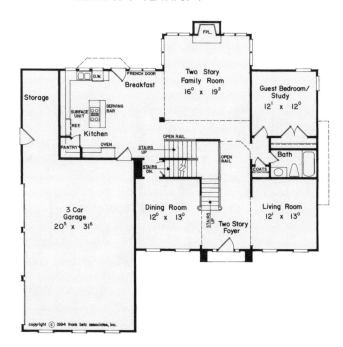

EASILY GRABBING THE UNDIVIDED attention of any passerby this well-structured facade is an example of affluent living. Behind the exterior, the second-floor master suite is magnetizing with its private vaulted bath, expanded walk-in closet and sitting area. Three family bedrooms, two full baths and an overlook are also on the second floor. The cooktop-island kitchen provides a walk-in pantry and an abundance of counter space—it is also open to the breakfast area. Storage space is available in the three-car garage.

THIS MAGNIFICENT ESTATE is detailed with exterior charm: a porte cochere connecting the detached garage to the house, a covered terrace and oval windows. The first floor consists of a lavish master suite, a cozy library with a fireplace, a grand room/solarium combination and an elegant formal dining room with another fireplace. Three bedrooms dominate the second floor—each features a walk-in closet. For the kids, there is a playroom and up another flight of stairs is a room for future expansion into a deluxe studio with a fireplace. Over the three-car garage, there is a room for a future mother-in-law or maid's suite. This home is designed with a walkout basement foundation.

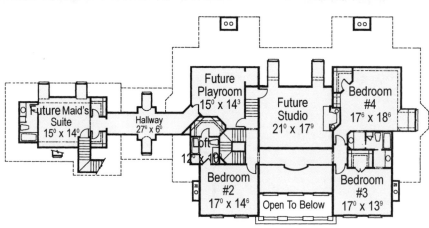

Future Maid's Suite 15⁰ x 14⁰

Hallway 27⁶ x 6⁰

Future Playroom 15⁰ x 14³

Future Studio 21⁰ x 17⁹

Bedroom #4 17⁶ x 18⁶

Loft 12 x 10

Bedroom #2 17⁰ x 14⁶

Open To Below

Bedroom #3 17⁰ x 13⁹

QUOTE ONE®
Cost to build? See page 214
to order complete cost estimate
to build this house in your area!

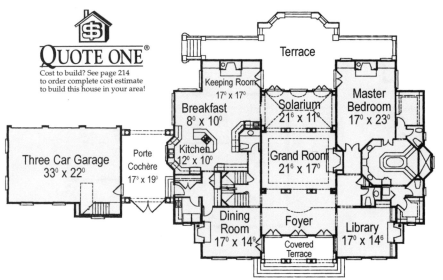

Three Car Garage 33⁰ x 22⁰

Porte Cochère 17³ x 19⁰

Terrace

Keeping Room 17⁰ x 17⁰

Breakfast 8⁰ x 10⁰

Kitchen 12⁰ x 10⁰

Solarium 21⁰ x 11⁰

Master Bedroom 17⁰ x 23⁰

Grand Room 21⁶ x 17⁰

Dining Room 17⁰ x 14⁹

Foyer

Library 17⁰ x 14⁶

Covered Terrace

DESIGN HPT740131

TOTAL: 5,130 square feet

FIRST FLOOR: 3,703 square feet

SECOND FLOOR: 1,427 square feet

BONUS SPACE: 1,399 square feet

BEDROOMS: 4

BATHROOMS: 3½ +½

WIDTH: 125'-2" DEPTH: 58'-10"

Homes with a dash of the past

DESIGN HPT740132

TOTAL: 4,465 square feet
FIRST FLOOR: 2,670 square feet
SECOND FLOOR: 1,795 square feet
FUTURE SPACE: 744 square feet
BEDROOMS: 5
BATHROOMS: 4½ +½
WIDTH: 74'-8" **DEPTH:** 93'-10"

REST YOUR EYES UPON this distinguishing two-story portico that directs the way to a pampering design. Just off the foyer, quiet time is accomplished in the library with a corner hearth. Nearby is the lavish master bedroom, which features a second fireplace, His and Her closets and an exquisite master bath. Wood beams, a third fireplace and a built-in entertainment center reveal the family room's true elegance. The kitchen contains a breakfast bar and area adjacent to the mud room and utility room. Four spacious bedrooms, a lounge and three full baths occupy the second floor.

DESIGN HPT740133

TOTAL: 6,061 square feet

FIRST FLOOR: 3,902 square feet

SECOND FLOOR: 2,159 square feet

BEDROOMS: 5

BATHROOMS: 3½

WIDTH: 85'-3" **DEPTH:** 74'-0"

THE ENTRY TO this classic home is framed with a sweeping double staircase and four large columns topped with a pediment. The two-story foyer is flanked by spacious living and dining rooms. Beyond the foyer, the home is designed with rooms that offer maximum livability. The two-story family room, which has a central fireplace, opens to the study and a solarium. A spacious U-shaped kitchen features a central island cooktop. An additional staircase off the breakfast room offers convenient access to the second floor. The impressive master suite features backyard access and a bath fit for royalty. A walk-in closet with an ironing board will provide room for everything. Four bedrooms upstairs enjoy large proportions. This home is designed with a walkout basement foundation.

DESIGN HPT740134

TOTAL: 4,304 square feet

FIRST FLOOR: 2,938 square feet

SECOND FLOOR: 1,366 square feet

BEDROOMS: 5

BATHROOMS: 3½

WIDTH: 107'-10" **DEPTH:** 51'-7"

THIS FEDERAL COLONIAL-STYLE HOME is distinguished by a front porch with decorative round columns. The side three-car garage opens to the utility room, the island worktop kitchen and the dining room. The gallery hall connects the dining room to the family gathering areas, which provide a scenic view of the outside patio and pool. The study is located next to the master suite. Upstairs, two full baths and four additional bedrooms—each one with a walk-in closet—provide sleeping quarters for the whole family.

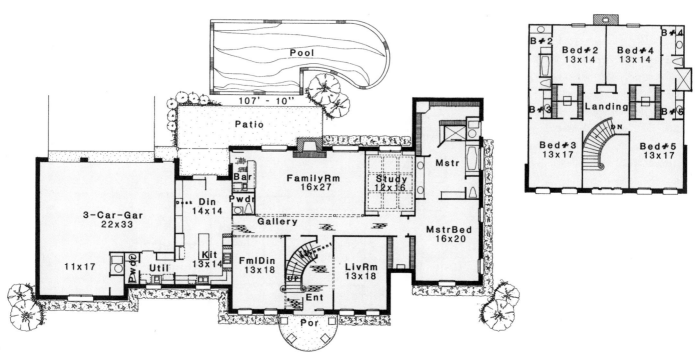

DESIGN HPT740135

TOTAL: 5,827 square feet

FIRST FLOOR: 4,082 square feet

SECOND FLOOR: 1,745 square feet

BEDROOMS: 7

BATHROOMS: 5½

WIDTH: 101'-7" **DEPTH:** 73'-0"

A GRACEFUL PALLADIAN-STYLE ENTRY with fluted, two-story columns commands charm and respect for this Georgian homestead. Inside, a marble entry provides a traditional circular stairway and balcony. To the left lies an inviting living room and a family room that includes a fireplace and atrium doors leading to the deck area and beyond. The large kitchen, formal dining room with bay window, bar area and expansive sun room provide more than enough space for entertaining guests. An exercise room is featured for family fun and health. A luxurious master suite is positioned at the rear for seclusion, while a guest suite can be found just to the front. Five family bedrooms complete the second floor.

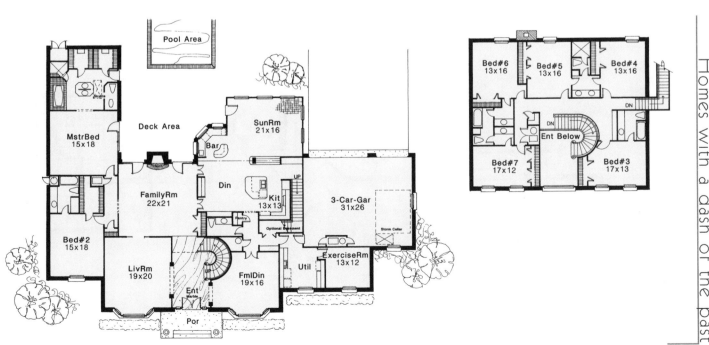

DESIGN HPT740136

TOTAL: 4,253 square feet

FIRST FLOOR: 3,335 square feet

SECOND FLOOR: 918 square feet

BEDROOMS: 4

BATHROOMS: 3½

WIDTH: 120'-5"   DEPTH: 82'-0"

SPORTING A TRADITIONAL GEORGIAN EXTERIOR, this home has an elegance of its own. A circular staircase highlights the two-story entry. The living room features a ten-foot ceiling and fireplace, while the adjoining study has a built-in wet bar and access to the rear deck. The large kitchen has a center island and brick trim along the cooktop and oven. The informal dining area opens to a private patio. A beamed cathedral ceiling and fireplace are focal points in the family room. The master suite is complete with a vaulted bedroom ceiling, fireplace and luxurious bath with His and Hers walk-in closets and vanities.

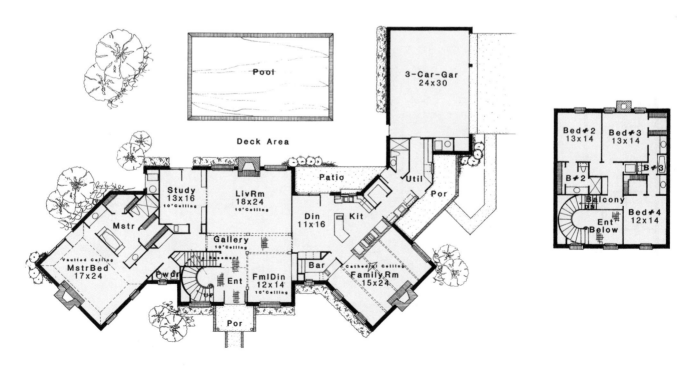

DESIGN HPT740137

TOTAL: 1,494 square feet

FIRST FLOOR: 759 square feet

SECOND FLOOR: 735 square feet

FINISHED BASEMENT: 759 square feet

BEDROOMS: 3

BATHROOMS: 1½

WIDTH: 22'-0" **DEPTH:** 36'-0"

THE CHARMING FRONT PORCH and the two-story turret welcome guests to this lovely home. The turret houses the living room on the first floor and the master suite on the second floor. The dining room is open to the living room and provides a box-bay window. The L-shaped kitchen features a breakfast room accessible to the backyard. A curved staircase next to the powder room leads upstairs to three bedrooms and a bath. Each family bedroom contains a walk-in closet. This home is designed with a basement foundation.

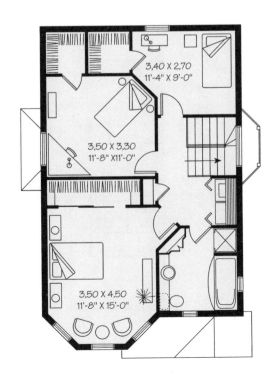

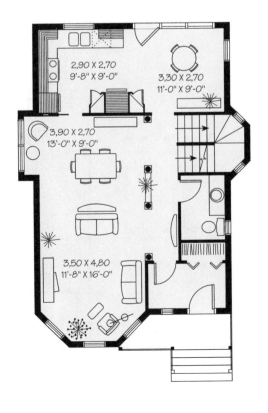

DESIGN HPT740138

TOTAL: 3,775 square feet

FIRST FLOOR: 1,901 square feet

SECOND FLOOR: 1,874 square feet

BEDROOMS: 4

BATHROOMS: 3½

WIDTH: 50'-0" DEPTH: 70'-0"

THIS ELEGANT CHARLESTON TOWNHOUSE is enhanced by Southern grace and three levels of charming livability. Covered porches offer outdoor living space at every level. The first floor offers a living room warmed by a fireplace, an island kitchen serving a bayed nook, and a formal dining room. A first-floor guest bedroom is located at the front of the plan, along with a laundry and powder room. The second level offers a sumptuous master suite boasting a private balcony, a master bath and enormous walk-in closet. Two other bedrooms sharing a Jack-and-Jill bath are also on this level. The basement level includes a three-car garage and game room warmed by a fireplace.

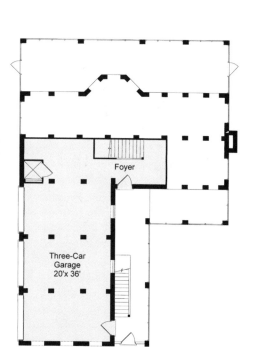

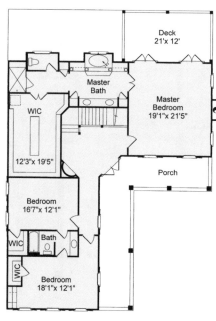

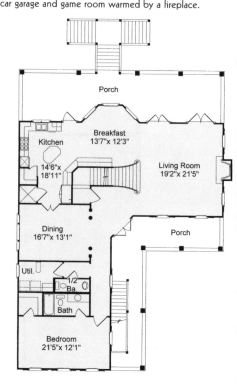

DESIGN HPT740139

TOTAL: 2,520 square feet

FIRST FLOOR: 1,305 square feet

SECOND FLOOR: 1,215 square feet

BONUS SPACE: 935 square feet

BEDROOMS: 3

BATHROOMS: 3

WIDTH: 30'-6" **DEPTH:** 72'-2"

THIS ELEGANT OLD CHARLESTON ROW design blends high vogue with a restful character that says shoes are optional. A flexible interior enjoys modern space that welcomes sunlight. Wraparound porticos on two levels offer views to the living areas, while a "sit and watch the stars" observation deck opens from the master suite. Four sets of French doors bring the outside in to the great room. The second-floor master suite features a spacious bath and three sets of doors that open to the observation deck. A guest bedroom on this level leads to a gallery hall with its own access to the deck. Bonus space awaits development on the lower level, which—true to its Old Charleston roots—opens gloriously to a garden courtyard.

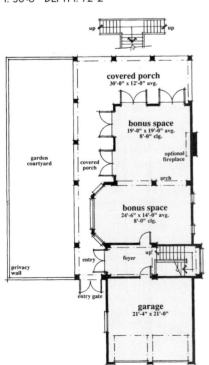

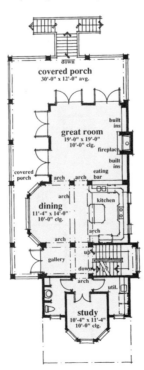

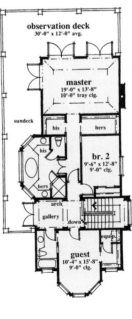

DESIGN HPT740140

TOTAL: 1,962 square feet

FIRST FLOOR: 904 square feet

SECOND FLOOR: 1,058 square feet

BEDROOMS: 3

BATHROOMS: 2½

WIDTH: 22'-0" DEPTH: 74'-0"

REMINISCENT OF THE popular "shotgun" homes of the past, this fine clapboard home is perfect for urban or riverfront living. Two balconies grace the second floor—one at the front and one on the side. A two-way fireplace between the formal living and dining rooms provides visual impact. Built-in bookcases flank an arched opening between these rooms. A pass-through from the kitchen to the dining room simplifies serving, and a walk-in pantry provides storage. On the second floor, the master bedroom opens to a large balcony, and the relaxing master bath is designed with a separate shower and an angled whirlpool tub. Two secondary bedrooms and a full bath are located at the rear of the plan. Please specify crawlspace or slab foundation when ordering.

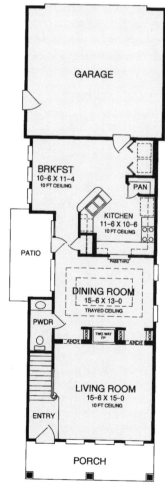

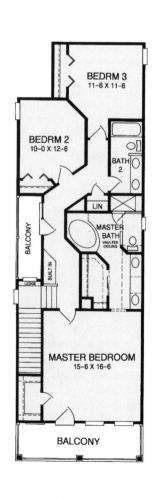

DESIGN HPT740141

TOTAL: 1,940 square feet

FIRST FLOOR: 911 square feet

SECOND FLOOR: 1,029 square feet

BEDROOMS: 3

BATHROOMS: 2½

WIDTH: 20'-10" DEPTH: 75'-10"

WITH IRRESISTIBLE CHARM and quiet curb appeal, this enchanting cottage conceals a sophisticated interior that's prepared for busy lifestyles. Built-in cabinetry in the great room frames a massive fireplace, which warms the area and complements the natural views. An open kitchen provides an island with a double sink and snack counter. Planned events are easily served in the formal dining room with French doors that lead to the veranda. On the upper level, a central hall with linen storage connects the sleeping quarters. The master suite boasts a walk-in closet and a roomy bath with a dual-sink vanity. Each of two secondary bedrooms has plenty of wardrobe space. Bedroom 3 leads out to the upper-level deck.

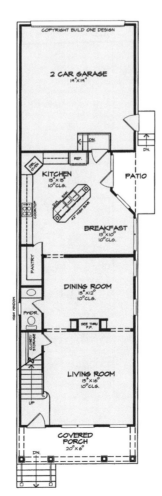

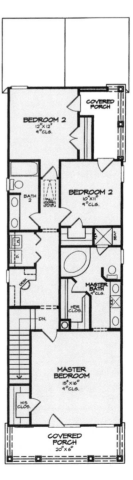

DESIGN HPT740142

TOTAL: 1,999 square feet

FIRST FLOOR: 1,078 square feet

SECOND FLOOR: 921 square feet

BEDROOMS: 3

BATHROOMS: 3

WIDTH: 24'-11" DEPTH: 73'-10"

THIS CHARMING CLAPBOARD home is loaded with character and is perfect for a narrow lot. Columns and connecting arches separate the great room and the dining room. The efficient U-shaped kitchen features a corner sink with a window view and a bayed breakfast area with access to the rear porch. A bedroom and a bath are conveniently located for guests on the first floor. Upstairs, the master suite features a vaulted ceiling and a luxurious bath with dual vanities, a whirlpool tub and a separate shower. A secondary bedroom and a full bath are also located on the second floor with a large rear balcony completing this highly livable plan. Please specify crawlspace or slab foundation when ordering.

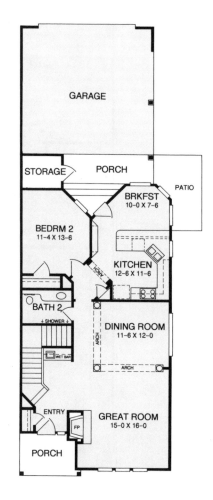

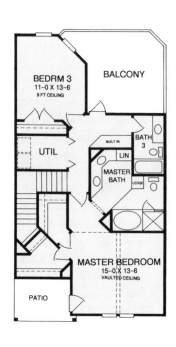

DESIGN HPT740143

TOTAL: 767 square feet

FIRST FLOOR: 512 square feet

SECOND FLOOR: 255 square feet

BEDROOMS: 1

BATHROOMS: 2

WIDTH: 30'-0" **DEPTH:** 32'-0"

DESIGNED FOR ONE PERSON or a couple, a vacation retreat or a year-round home, this 767-square-foot plan presents simple living with maximum comfort. The corner porch is vast enough for a pair of rocking chairs, and inside, the two-story living room is cozy with a fireplace flanked by windows. The island kitchen boasts a box-bay nook, perfect for every meal of the day. The second floor is dedicated to the master bedroom, which includes a private bath and His and Hers wardrobes.

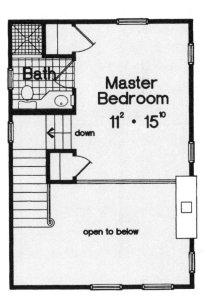

DESIGN HPT740144

TOTAL: 1,445 square feet

FIRST FLOOR: 685 square feet

SECOND FLOOR: 760 square feet

BEDROOMS: 2½

BATHROOMS: 1½

WIDTH: 21'-0" DEPTH: 36'-0"

ON THIS PLAN, the garage is under the rear of the house. This is designed for a narrow lot or to be joined with other townhouses to form a set. The basic version is complete by itself, while the enhanced version has exterior details such as gables and a box-bay window. The first floor features an efficient kitchen with a snack bar, a powder room and a combined living room/dining room with an optional fireplace. Upstairs are a private master suite, two bedrooms sharing a bath and a convenient laundry room.

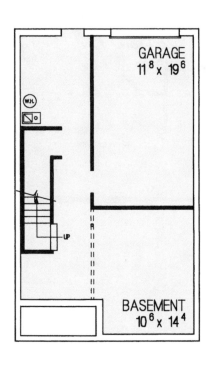

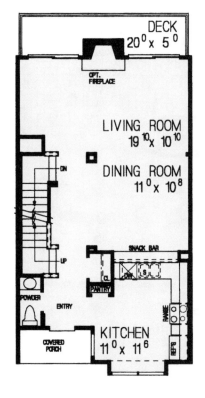

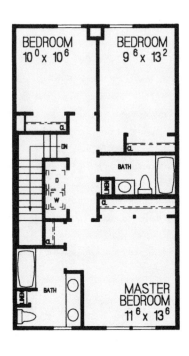

DESIGN HPT740145

TOTAL: 1,910 square feet

FIRST FLOOR: 873 square feet

SECOND FLOOR: 1,037 square feet

BEDROOMS: 3

BATHROOMS: 2½

WIDTH: 27'-6" DEPTH: 64'-0"x

THIS EFFICIENT SALTBOX design includes three bedrooms and two full baths, plus a handy powder room on the first floor. A large great room at the front of the home features a fireplace. The rear of the home is left open, with room for the kitchen with a snack bar, the breakfast area with a fireplace, and the dining room with outdoor access. If you wish, use the breakfast area as an all-purpose dining room and turn the dining room into a library or sitting room. Upstairs, the vaulted master suite accesses its own private sun deck and a full bath, while two additional second-floor bedrooms share a full bath.

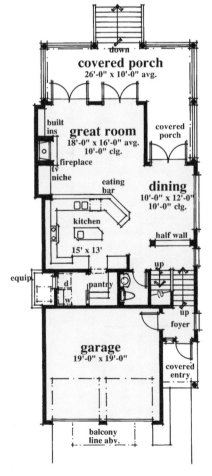

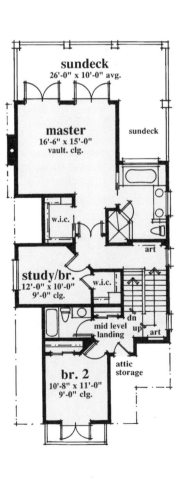

REAR VIEW

A PALLADIAN WINDOW adds interest to the modified-gable roofline of this livable three-bedroom design. Columns and tall glass panels flank the covered entryway. A hall closet and a powder room line the foyer. The great room includes a warming fireplace, and the kitchen and the breakfast area with patio access sit across the back. The master suite with a deluxe private bath and walk-in closet, plus the two family bedrooms, resides on the second floor. Please specify crawlspace or slab foundation when ordering.

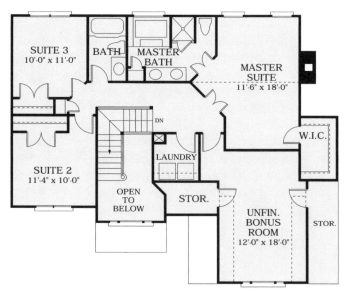

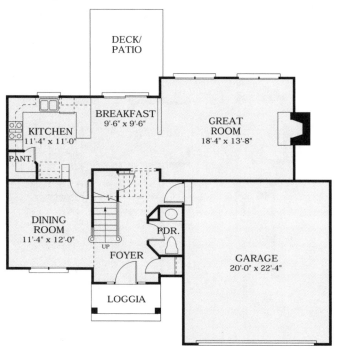

DESIGN HPT740146

TOTAL: 1,719 square feet

FIRST FLOOR: 844 square feet

SECOND FLOOR: 875 square feet

BONUS SPACE: 242 square feet

BEDROOMS: 3

BATHROOMS: 2½

WIDTH: 45'-0" DEPTH: 37'-0"

DESIGN HPT740147

TOTAL: 3,059 square feet

FIRST FLOOR: 1,527 square feet

SECOND FLOOR: 1,532 square feet

BEDROOMS: 4

BATHROOMS: 3½

WIDTH: 44'-4" **DEPTH:** 55'-0"

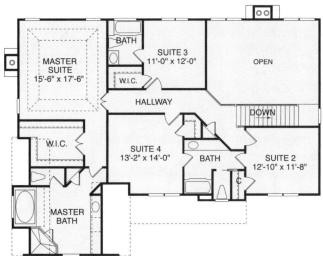

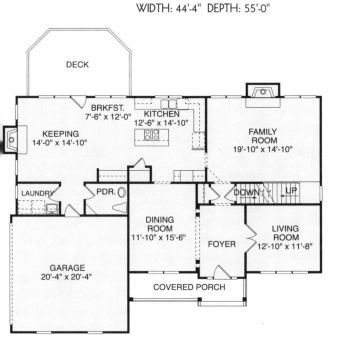

A CHARMING COVERED PORCH shelters the entrance to this happy French garden design. With the formal living room and dining room at the front, the foyer leads through double doors to the family room with a fireplace flanked by tall windows. The island kitchen blends seamlessly with the breakfast area and large keeping room, which has a fireplace and access to the rear deck. An angled hallway on the second level, overlooking the family room below, connects three bedrooms with adjoining baths and the master suite with its vaulted ceiling, an oversized walk-in closet and garden tub. Please specify basement or crawlspace foundation.

DESIGN HPT740148

TOTAL: 2,024 square feet

FIRST FLOOR: 1,147 square feet

SECOND FLOOR: 877 square feet

BONUS SPACE: 193 square feet

BEDROOMS: 3

BATHROOMS: 2½

WIDTH: 50'-0" DEPTH: 41'-10"

Quote One®

Cost to build? See page 214
to order complete cost estimate
to build this house in your area!

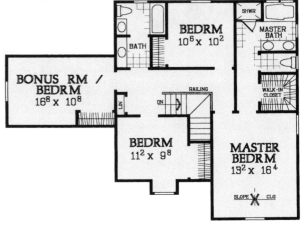

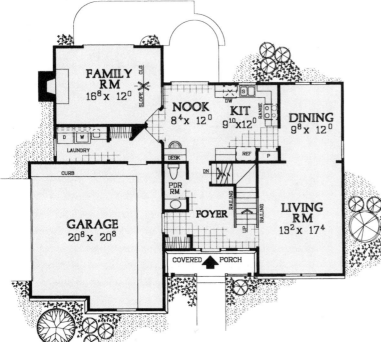

THIS HOME FEATURES a covered porch that bids welcome into an interior that lends itself to quiet casual living or to entertaining with style. The floor plan offers a large living room that leads to the rear dining room and kitchen. A large family room with a cozy fireplace and a convenient laundry room are found nearby. On the second floor, the master bedroom provides ample room for furniture placement and features an amenity-filled master bath with a separate shower and tub, dual sinks and a walk-in closet. Three family bedrooms—or two bedrooms and a bonus room—share a full bath with separate sinks.

DESIGN HPT740149

TOTAL: 2,037 square feet

FIRST FLOOR: 1,160 square feet

SECOND FLOOR: 877 square feet

BONUS SPACE: 193 square feet

BEDROOMS: 3

BATHROOMS: 2½

WIDTH: 50'-0" **DEPTH:** 43'-6"

Quote One®

Cost to build? See page 214
to order complete cost estimate
to build this house in your area!

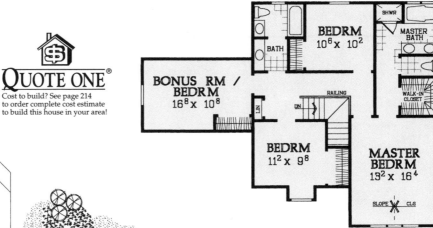

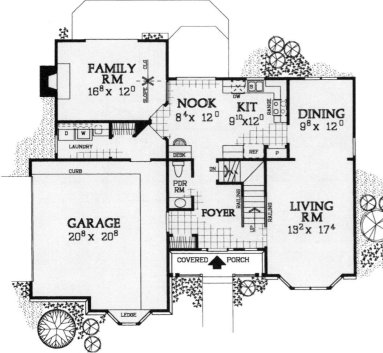

THIS CHARMING HOME offers two bay windows that bathe the foyer with natural light and set the tone for the warmth and comfort found throughout. The L-shaped kitchen contains a pantry and an adjacent nook, while the nearby dining room flows through to the living room. The family room provides a fireplace and access to the rear yard. On the second floor is the master bedroom with a private bath and a walk-in closet, as well as two bedrooms—or make it a fourth bedroom—and a full hall bath. The utility room resides near the garage entrance.

GRACEFUL COLUMNS AND MULTI-PANE WINDOWS frame the entrance to this understated two-story

contemporary design. The view from the foyer extends through the gathering room and out onto the covered veranda. The dining room with bay window to the left of the foyer connects to the kitchen with angled bar and corner breakfast nook. The first-floor master suite has a bay window, perfect for a writing desk, and a garden tub in the bath. Versatile club quarters share the second level with two additional bedrooms and a full bath. Also on this level, a large room with walk-in closet is available as a fourth bedroom or home office.

DESIGN HPT740150

TOTAL: 2,552 square feet
FIRST FLOOR: 1,635 square feet
SECOND FLOOR: 917 square feet
BONUS SPACE: 271 square feet
BEDROOMS: 3
BATHROOMS: 2½
WIDTH: 46'-10" DEPTH: 60'-10"

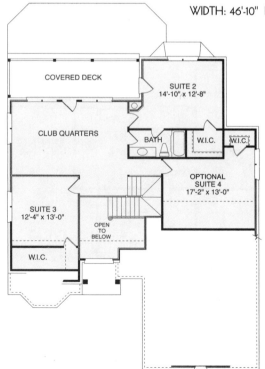

DESIGN HPT740151

SQUARE FOOTAGE: 1,915

BEDROOMS: 3

BATHROOMS: 2

WIDTH: 45'-10" DEPTH: 62'-6"

CHOOSE THREE BEDROOMS or two bedrooms plus a den in this single-level contemporary design. The well-equipped kitchen is open to a large dining room that overlooks the deck just beyond. The gathering room with a sloped ceiling also has a wall of windows across the back and a fireplace in the side wall. The master suite features twin basins and a walk-in closet. Two other bedrooms with an adjoining bath reside off the entry foyer. One of these bedrooms may be used as a den.

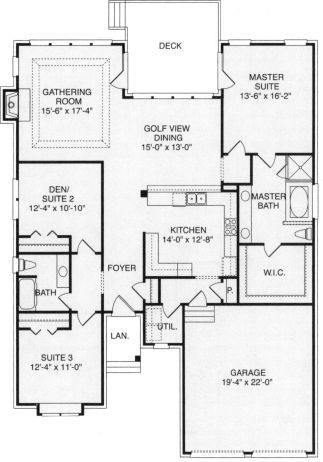

DECK

GATHERING
ROOM
15'-6" x 17'-4"

MASTER
SUITE
13'-6" x 16'-2"

GOLF VIEW
DINING
15'-0" x 13'-0"

DEN/
SUITE 2
12'-4" x 10'-10"

MASTER
BATH

KITCHEN
14'-0" x 12'-8"

FOYER

W.I.C.

BATH

P.

UTIL.

LAN.

GARAGE
19'-4" x 22'-0"

SUITE 3
12'-4" x 11'-0"

Homes for town centers

159

DESIGN HPT740152

TOTAL: 1,681 square feet

FIRST FLOOR: 852 square feet

SECOND FLOOR: 829 square feet

BONUS SPACE: 359 square feet

BEDROOMS: 3

BATHROOMS: 2½

WIDTH: 50'-0" DEPTH: 36'-0"

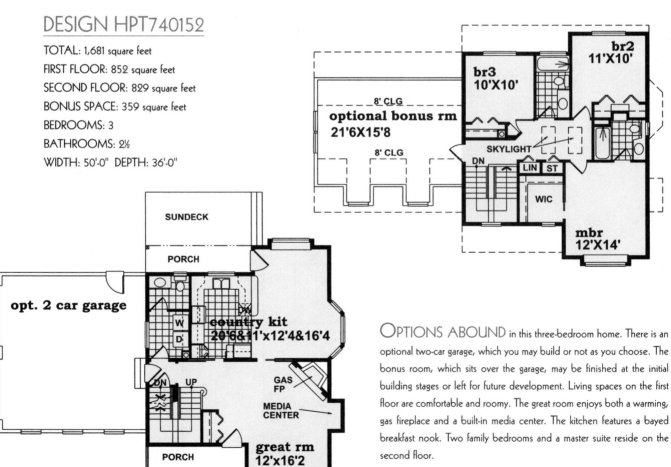

OPTIONS ABOUND in this three-bedroom home. There is an optional two-car garage, which you may build or not as you choose. The bonus room, which sits over the garage, may be finished at the initial building stages or left for future development. Living spaces on the first floor are comfortable and roomy. The great room enjoys both a warming gas fireplace and a built-in media center. The kitchen features a bayed breakfast nook. Two family bedrooms and a master suite reside on the second floor.

DESIGN HPT740153

TOTAL: 1,776 square feet

FIRST FLOOR: 891 square feet

SECOND FLOOR: 885 square feet

BEDROOMS: 4

BATHROOMS: 2½

WIDTH: 44'-0"   DEPTH: 40'-0"

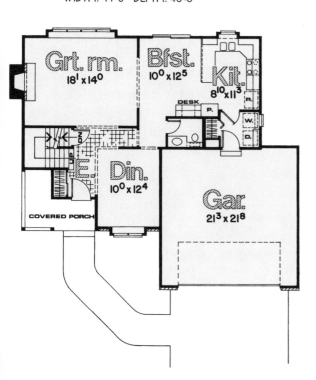

THE INVITING WRAPAROUND front porch of this home leads to a gracious entry with an interesting staircase. Immediately to the right is the formal dining room, featuring a box-bay window. Straight ahead, the great room—with a raised-hearth fireplace—opens to the breakfast room and kitchen. Windows over the sink and sliding glass doors to the rear yard let the outdoors in. Other special features on this floor include a powder room and a built-in planning desk in the kitchen. Four upstairs bedrooms include a master suite and three family bedrooms. The master suite provides ample closet space and a private whirlpool bath.

DECK

BREAKFAST
12'-6" x 12'-0"

GREAT
ROOM
16'-6" x 17'-6"

MASTER
SUITE
13'-6" x 16'-6"

KITCHEN
12'-6" x 15'-6"

W.I.C.

DINING
ROOM
12'-0" x 12'-4"

FOYER

PDR.

UP

MASTER
BATH

LAUNDRY

PORTICO

GARAGE
21'-4" x 21'-4"

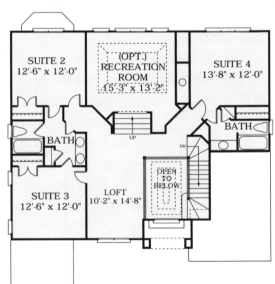

SUITE 2
12'-6" x 12'-0"

(OPT.)
RECREATION
ROOM
15'-3" x 13'-2"

SUITE 4
13'-8" x 12'-0"

BATH

BATH

UP

DN

OPEN
TO
BELOW

SUITE 3
12'-6" x 12'-0"

LOFT
10'-2" x 14'-8"

DESIGN HPT740154

TOTAL: 2,794 square feet

FIRST FLOOR: 1,751 square feet

SECOND FLOOR: 1,043 square feet

BEDROOMS: 4

BATHROOMS: 3½

WIDTH: 45'-0" DEPTH: 69'-6"

STATELY PILASTERS and a decorative balcony at a second-level window adorn this ornate four-bedroom design. Inside, columns define the formal dining room. Ahead is a great room with a fireplace, built-in bookshelves and access to the rear deck. A breakfast nook nestles in a bay window and joins an efficient island kitchen. The master suite on the first level has a tray ceiling and a walk-in closet and garden tub in the bath. Upstairs, a versatile loft, three additional bedrooms and two baths are connected by a hallway open to the great room below.

DESIGN HPT740155

TOTAL: 2,590 square feet

FIRST FLOOR: 1,266 square feet

SECOND FLOOR: 1,324 square feet

BEDROOMS: 3

BATHROOMS: 2½

WIDTH: 34'-0" DEPTH: 63'-2"

THIS LOVELY contemporary home boasts plenty of indoor/outdoor flow. Four sets of double doors wrap around the great room and dining area and open to the stunning veranda. The great room is enhanced by a coffered ceiling and built-in cabinetry, while the entire first floor is bathed in sunlight from a wall of glass doors overlooking the veranda. The dining room connects to a gourmet island kitchen. Upstairs, a beautiful deck wraps gracefully around the family bedrooms. The master suite is a skylit haven enhanced by a sitting bay, which features a vaulted octagonal ceiling and a cozy two-sided fireplace. Private double doors access the sun deck from the master suite, the secondary bedrooms and the study.

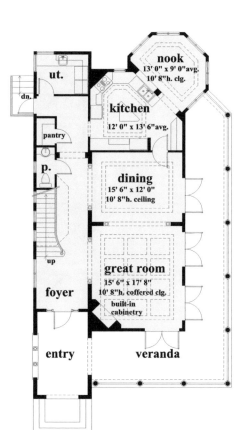

Sun-loving homes for entertaining

163

J.N. HANSEN S.D.G.

ONLY FIFTY FEET IN WIDTH, this fabulous design will fit anywhere! From the moment you enter the home from the foyer, this floor plan explodes in every direction with huge living spaces. Flanking the foyer are the living and dining rooms, and the visual impact of the staircase is breathtaking. Two-story ceilings adorn the huge family room with double-stacked glass walls. Sunlight floods the breakfast nook, and the kitchen is a gourmet's dream, complete with a cooking island and loads of overhead cabinets. Tray ceilings grace the master suite, which also offers a well-designed private bath. Here, a large soaking tub, doorless shower, private toilet chamber and huge walk-in closet are sure to please. Upstairs, two oversized bedrooms and a loft space—perfect for the home computer—share a full bath.

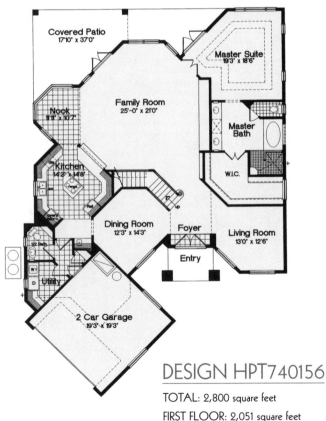

DESIGN HPT740156

TOTAL: 2,800 square feet

FIRST FLOOR: 2,051 square feet

SECOND FLOOR: 749 square feet

BEDROOMS: 3

BATHROOMS: 2½

WIDTH: 50'-0"   DEPTH: 74'-0"

DESIGN HPT740157

TOTAL: 2,729 square feet

FIRST FLOOR: 2,365 square feet

SECOND FLOOR: 364 square feet

BEDROOMS: 3

BATHROOMS: 3

WIDTH: 69'-0" DEPTH: 70'-0"

THE COLUMNED FOYER of this home welcomes you into a series of spaces that reach out in all directions. The living room has a spectacular view of the huge covered patio area that's perfect for summer entertaining. The dining room features a tray ceiling and French doors that lead to a covered porch. A secluded master suite affords great views through French doors and also has a tray ceiling. The family wing combines an island kitchen, nook and family gathering space, with the built-in media/fireplace wall the center of attention. Two secondary bedrooms share a bath. A staircase overlooking the family room takes you up to the sun room complete with a full bath.

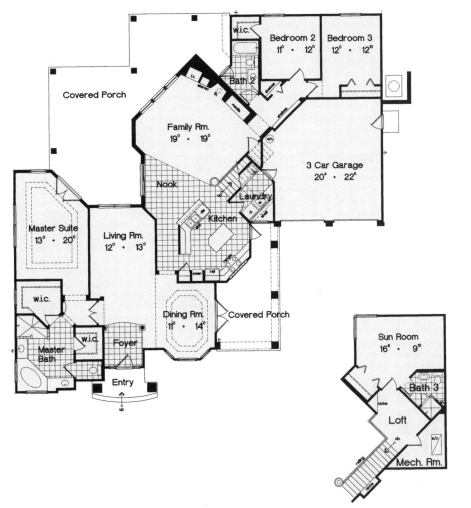

DESIGN HPT740158

TOTAL: 4,084 square feet

MAIN LEVEL: 2,262 square feet

LOWER LEVEL: 1,822 square feet

BEDROOMS: 4

BATHROOMS: 3½

WIDTH: 109'-11" DEPTH: 46'-0"

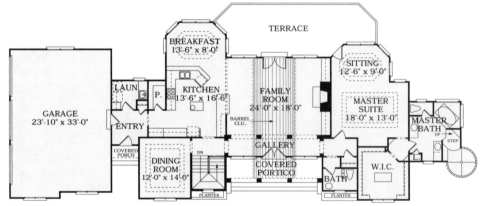

TERRACE

GARAGE
23'-10" x 33'-0"

LAUN

ENTRY

COVERED
PORCH

BREAKFAST
13'-6" x 8'-0"

P.

KITCHEN
13'-6" x 16'-6"

DINING
ROOM
12'-0" x 14'-0"

DN

PLANTER

FAMILY
ROOM
24'-0" x 18'-0"

BARREL
CLG.

GALLERY

COVERED
PORTICO

SITTING
12'-6" x 9'-0"

MASTER
SUITE
18'-0" x 13'-0"

MASTER
BATH

UP
STEP

BATH

W.I.C.

PLANTER

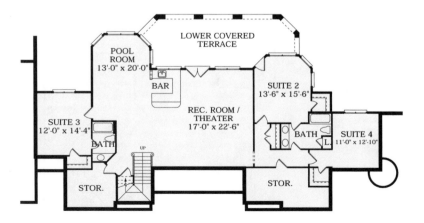

LOWER COVERED
TERRACE

POOL
ROOM
13'-0" x 20'-0"

BAR

SUITE 3
12'-0" x 14'-4"

BATH

UP

STOR.

REC. ROOM /
THEATER
17'-0" x 22'-6"

SUITE 2
13'-6" x 15'-6"

BATH

L

SUITE 4
11'-0" x 12'-10"

STOR.

THIS EXQUISITE HOME is definitely Mediterranean, with its corner quoins, lintels and tall entry. This home features a dining room, a massive family room with a fireplace, a gourmet kitchen with a breakfast area, and a laundry room. Finishing the first floor is a lavish master suite which enjoys a vast walk-in closet, a sitting area and a pampering private bath. The lower level features three suites, two full baths, a pool room and a recreation room/theater along with two storage rooms.

THE TOWERING ENTRY of this stucco beauty makes for a gracious entrance to the floor plan inside. Double doors open off the covered front porch to a dining room and a living room defined by columns. A fireplace warms the living room. To the back are the casual areas: a family room, breakfast nook and gourmet kitchen. A bedroom with a full bath and the utility area sit directly behind the two-car garage. The master suite features a study and private bath. The lower level can be developed into a recreation room or additional bedroom suites.

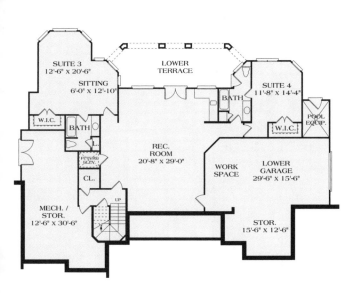

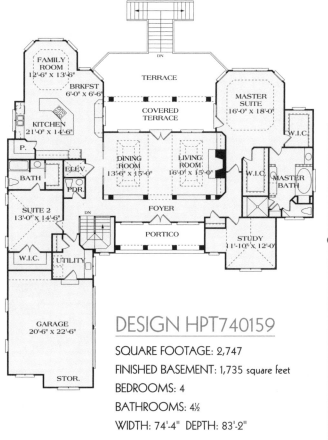

DESIGN HPT740159

SQUARE FOOTAGE: 2,747

FINISHED BASEMENT: 1,735 square feet

BEDROOMS: 4

BATHROOMS: 4½

WIDTH: 74'-4" DEPTH: 83'-2"

Sun-loving homes for entertaining

DESIGN HPT740160

TOTAL: 3,709 square feet

FIRST FLOOR: 2,538 square feet

SECOND FLOOR: 1,171 square feet

FINISHED BASEMENT: 1,784 square feet

BEDROOMS: 4

BATHROOMS: 3½

WIDTH: 67'-7" **DEPTH:** 85'-1"

THIS IMPRESSIVE MEDITERRANEAN design is dazzled in Italianate style. A front portico offers a warm welcome into the main level. The master suite is located to the left and includes rear-deck access, a double walk-in closet and pampering master bath. The island kitchen serves the formal and casual dining areas with ease. The casual gathering area is warmed by a fireplace. Three additional family suites reside upstairs, along with two baths and a balcony overlooking the two-story living room. The basement level adds a whole new layer of luxury, offering an additional suite, game room, recreation room, lounge area, wet bar and unfinished workshop and mechanical space for future use.

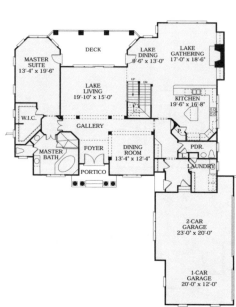

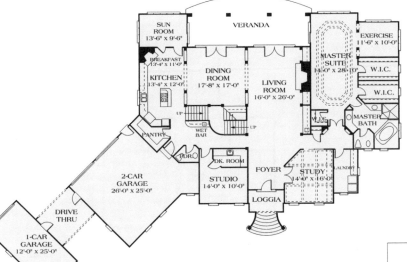

SUN ROOM
13'-6" X 9'-6"

VERANDA

EXERCISE
11'-6" X 10'-0"

BREAKFAST
13'-4" X 11'-0"

MASTER
SUITE
14'-0" X 28'-10"

W.I.C.

KITCHEN
13'-4" X 12'-0"

DINING
ROOM
17'-8" X 17'-0"

LIVING
ROOM
16'-0" X 26'-0"

W.I.C.

PANTRY

UP

WET
BAR

UP

W.I.C.

MASTER
BATH

PDR.

DK. ROOM

FOYER

STUDY
14'-0" X 16'-0"

LAUNDRY

2-CAR
GARAGE
26'-0" X 25'-0"

STUDIO
14'-0" X 10'-0"

LOGGIA

DRIVE
THRU

1-CAR
GARAGE
12'-0" X 25'-0"

DESIGN HPT740161

TOTAL: 4,928 square feet

FIRST FLOOR: 3,562 square feet

SECOND FLOOR: 1,366 square feet

BONUS SPACE: 957 square feet

BEDROOMS: 3

BATHROOMS: 3½

WIDTH: 134'-8" DEPTH: 89'-8"

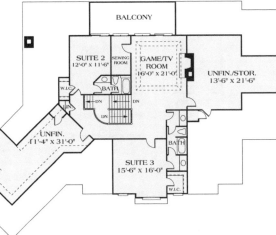

BALCONY

SUITE 2
12'-0" X 11'-6"

SEWING
ROOM

GAME/TV
ROOM
16'-0" X 21'-0"

UNFIN./STOR.
13'-6" X 21'-6"

W.I.C.

BATH

DN

DN

LIN

DN

UNFIN.
11'-4" X 31'-0"

BATH

SUITE 3
15'-6" X 16'-0"

W.I.C.

MAKING A GRAND ENTRANCE is almost required with this fine two-story stucco home. The elegant loggia leads to the foyer where a beam-ceilinged study waits on the right. Directly ahead is a wonderfully large living room, complete with a warming fireplace, built-ins and access to the rear veranda. A spacious formal dining room also offers access to the veranda and is easily serviced by the large island kitchen. Note the studio—with a built-in darkroom—at the front of the home. The deluxe master suite is designed to pamper. Upstairs, two suites offer private baths and walk-in closets. A game/TV room is enhanced by a third fireplace and sits adjacent to a sewing room. There are two large unfinished rooms completing this floor.

Sun-loving homes for entertaining

DESIGN HPT740162

TOTAL: 2,600 square feet

FIRST FLOOR: 1,679 square feet

SECOND FLOOR: 921 square feet

BEDROOMS: 4

BATHROOMS: 2½

WIDTH: 58'-0" DEPTH: 58'-10"

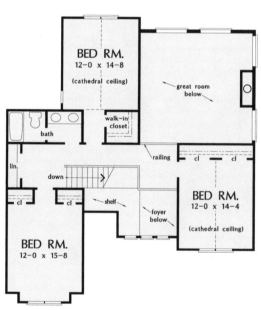

THIS MEDITERRANEAN-STYLE beauty is not just a fresh face—its well-planned interior provides all of the flexibility that the new age requires. An open two-story great room boasts a fireplace and access to the rear covered porch. The U-shaped kitchen provides a convenient pass-through shared with the great room. A triple window brightens the breakfast area, which also features access to the rear porch. Gorgeous amenities enhance the master suite, including a coffered ceiling and a bay window. Upstairs, three secondary bedrooms share a balcony hall that leads to a full bath.

DESIGN HPT740163

TOTAL: 2,097 square feet

FIRST FLOOR: 1,065 square feet

SECOND FLOOR: 1,032 square feet

BEDROOMS: 4

BATHROOMS: 2½

WIDTH: 38'-0" **DEPTH:** 38'-0"

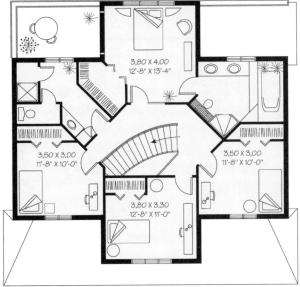

THIS MEDITERRANEAN HOME offers a dreamy living-by-the-water lifestyle, but it's ready to build in any region. A lovely arch-top entry announces an exquisite foyer with a curved staircase. The family room provides a fireplace and opens to the outdoors on both sides of the plan. An L-shaped kitchen serves a cozy morning area as well as a stunning formal dining room, which offers a bay window. Second-floor sleeping quarters include four bedrooms and two bathrooms. The master suite opens to a balcony and offers a bath with a double-bowl vanity. This home is designed with a basement foundation.

DESIGN HPT740164

TOTAL: 3,338 square feet

FIRST FLOOR: 1,989 square feet

SECOND FLOOR: 1,349 square feet

FINISHED BASEMENT: 105 square feet

BONUS SPACE: 487 square feet

BEDROOMS: 3

BATHROOMS: 2½

WIDTH: 63'-0" **DEPTH:** 48'-0"

DRAMATIC BALCONIES and spectacular window treatments enhance this stunning luxury home. Inside, a through-fireplace warms the formal living room and a restful den. Both living spaces open to a balcony that invites quiet reflection on starry nights. The banquet-sized dining room is easily served from the adjacent kitchen. Here, space is shared with an eating nook that provides access to the rear grounds and a family room with a corner fireplace—perfect for casual gatherings. The upper level contains two family bedrooms and a luxurious master suite that enjoys its own private balcony. The lower level accommodates a shop and a bonus room for future development.

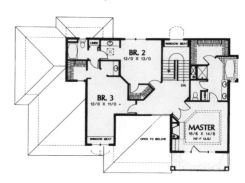

Cost to build? See page 214
to order complete cost estimate
to build this house in your area!

DESIGN HPT740165

SQUARE FOOTAGE: 2,397

BEDROOMS: 3

BATHROOMS: 2½

WIDTH: 73'-2" DEPTH: 73'-2"

DRAMATIC ROOFLINES and a unique entrance set the mood of this contemporary home. Double doors lead into the foyer, which opens directly to the formal living and dining rooms. A den/study is adjacent to this area and offers a quiet retreat. The spacious kitchen features a large cooktop work island and plenty of counter and cabinet space. The spacious family room expands this area and features a wall of windows and a warming fireplace. Two secondary bedrooms share a full bath. The master suite is designed with pleasure in mind. Included in the suite are a lavish bath and a deluxe walk-in closet, as well as access to the covered patio.

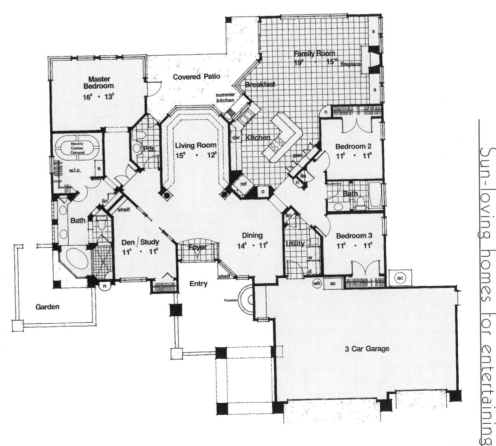

Master Bedroom
16⁸ · 13⁰

Covered Patio

Family Room
19⁴ · 15¹⁰ fireplace

Breakfast

summer kitchen

Electric Clothes Carousel

w.i.c.

Pdr.

Living Room
15⁸ · 12⁰

dw

Kitchen

par

Bedroom 2
11⁴ · 11⁰

Bath

shelf

lin

ref

o

Bath

Den / Study
11⁴ · 11⁰

Foyer

Dining
14⁰ · 11⁸

Utility

w

d

Bedroom 3
11⁰ · 11⁰

Garden

Entry

shelf

Fountain

wh

ac

ac

3 Car Garage

DESIGN HPT740166

SQUARE FOOTAGE: 2,978

BEDROOMS: 3

BATHROOMS: 3½

WIDTH: 84'-0" DEPTH: 90'-0"

THIS HOME IS DESIGNED to be a home-owner's dream come true. A formal living area opens from the gallery foyer through graceful arches and looks out to the veranda. The veranda hosts an outdoor grill and service counter—perfect for outdoor entertaining. The leisure room offers a private veranda, a cabana bath and a wet bar just off the gourmet kitchen. Walls of windows and a bayed breakfast nook let in natural light and set a bright tone for this area. The master suite opens to the rear property through French doors and boasts a lavish bath with a corner whirlpool tub that overlooks a private garden. An art niche off the gallery hall, a private dressing area and a secluded study complement the master suite. Two family bedrooms occupy the opposite wing of the plan and share a full bath and private hall.

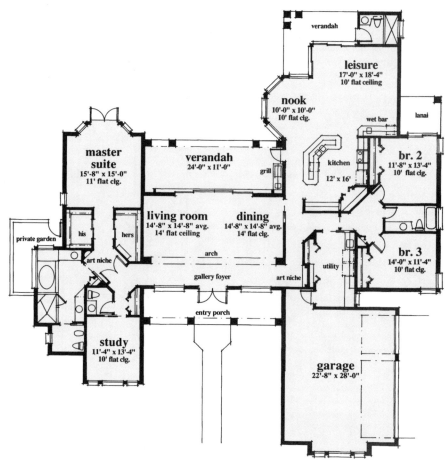

DESIGN HPT740167

SQUARE FOOTAGE: 2,831

BEDROOMS: 4

BATHROOMS: 3

WIDTH: 84'-0" DEPTH: 77'-0"

L

BESIDES GREAT CURB appeal, this home has a wonderful floor plan. The foyer features a fountain that greets visitors and leads to a formal dining room on the right and a living room on the left. A large family room at the rear has a built-in entertainment center and a fireplace. The U-shaped kitchen is perfectly located for servicing all living and dining areas. To the right of the plan, away from the central entertaining spaces, are three family bedrooms sharing a full bath. On the left side, with solitude and comfort for the master suite, are a large sitting area, an office and an amenity-filled bath. A deck with a spa sits outside the master suite.

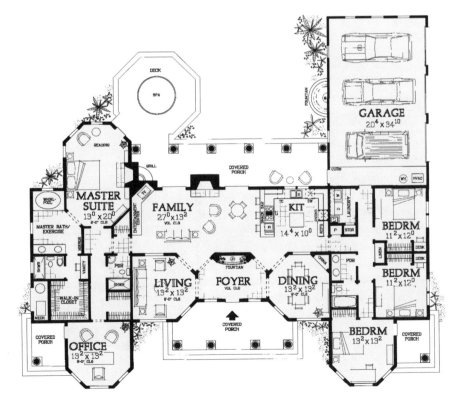

Sun-loving homes for entertaining

DESIGN HPT740168

SQUARE FOOTAGE: 2,348

BEDROOMS: 4

BATHROOMS: 3

WIDTH: 61'-4" DEPTH: 65'-0"

THIS HOME BOASTS great curb appeal with its Mediterranean influences—glass block and muntin windows, decorative oval window, impressive pillars and a stucco facade. The family side of this home abounds with thoughtful design features, like the island in the kitchen, the media/fireplace wall in the family room and the mitered glass breakfast nook. A dramatic arched entry into the master suite leads to a gently curving wall of glass block, a double vanity, extra large shower, compartmented toilet and large walk-in closet. Also special is the design of the three secondary bedrooms, which share private bath facilities. Bedrooms 3 and 4 share a popular "pullman" bath, while Bedroom 2 has access to the pool bath. With vaulted ceilings throughout most of this plan, an exciting living environment is guaranteed.

DESIGN HPT740169

SQUARE FOOTAGE: 2,456

BEDROOMS: 4

BATHROOMS: 3

WIDTH: 63'-8" DEPTH: 58'-0"

MULTI-PANED WINDOWS, a hipped roof and a columned, vaulted entry lend a Mediterranean aura to this four-bedroom home. Elegance continues inside with columns defining the living room and dining area. Entertaining will be easy in this sizable living room with a fireplace and built-in entertainment center. The master suite enjoys a tray ceiling, walk-in closet and sumptuous bath including dual vanity sinks, a garden tub set by a glass block window and separate shower. A guest suite with a private bath lies nearby. A bay-windowed breakfast nook features views of the rear covered patio and access to the convenient kitchen with a walk-in pantry. The two secondary bedrooms set to the right of the design share the pool bathroom. Note the learning center off the bedroom wing—a perfect place for the home computer.

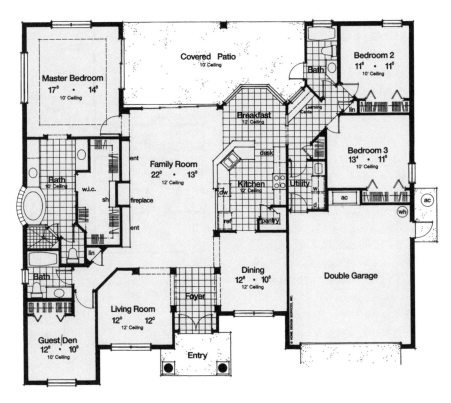

Sun-loving homes for entertaining

177

DESIGN HPT740170

SQUARE FOOTAGE: 2,388
BEDROOMS: 3
BATHROOMS: 2½
WIDTH: 63'-0" DEPTH: 60'-0"

QUOINS, ARCHED LINTELS and twin pedimented dormers lend this house a sweet country feel. Columns and a vaulted ceiling make the interior elegant. French doors lead to a living room found at the left of the entrance while decorative columns adorn the elegant dining room. The spacious family room is enhanced by the vaulted ceiling and cozy fireplace. Two lovely bay windows embellish the rear of the house. The island kitchen features a roomy pantry, a serving bar, and a breakfast area with a French door with a transom accessing outside. The master suite boasts a tray ceiling, sitting area, a deluxe bath with built-in plant shelves, a radius window, dual vanities, and a large walk-in closet. Please specify basement, crawlspace or slab foundation when ordering.

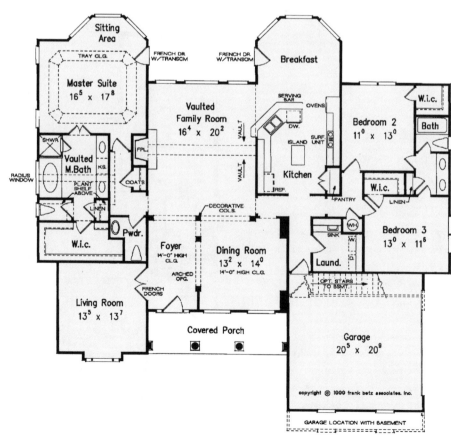

DESIGN HPT740171

SQUARE FOOTAGE: 3,566

BEDROOMS: 3

BATHROOMS: 2½

WIDTH: 88'-0" DEPTH: 70'-8"

SYMMETRICALLY GRAND, this home features large windows, which flood the interior with natural light. The massive sunken great room with a vaulted ceiling includes an exciting balcony overlook of the towering atrium window wall. The open breakfast nook and hearth room adjoin the kitchen. Four fireplaces throughout the house create an overall sense of warmth. A colonnade, a private entrance to the rear deck, and a sunken tub with a fireplace complement the master suite. Two family bedrooms share a dual-vanity bath.

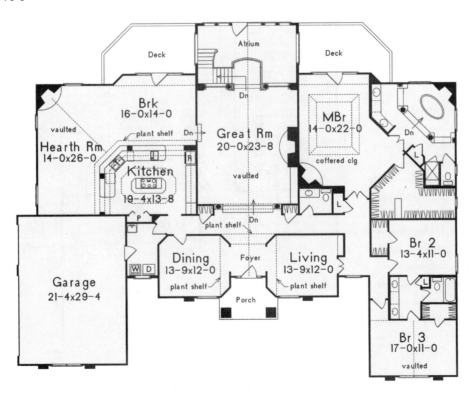

B. NATHAN

DESIGN HPT740172

SQUARE FOOTAGE: 1,954

BEDROOMS: 4

BATHROOMS: 2½

WIDTH: 64'-10" **DEPTH:** 58'-10"

DIRECT FROM THE Mediterranean, this Spanish-style, one-story home offers a practical floor plan. The facade features arch-top, multi-pane windows, a columned front porch, a tall chimney and a tiled roof. The interior has a wealth of livability. What you'll appreciate first is the juxtaposition of the great room and the formal dining room—both defined by columns. A more casual eating area is attached to the L-shaped kitchen and accesses a screened porch, as does the great room. Three bedrooms mean abundant sleeping space. The study could be a fourth bedroom—choose the full bath option in this case. A tray ceiling decorates the master suite, which is further enhanced by a bath with a separate shower and tub, walk-in closet and double sinks.

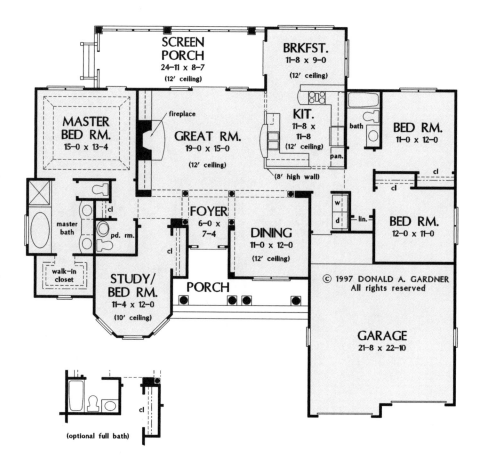

DESIGN HPT740173

SQUARE FOOTAGE: 1,932

BEDROOMS: 3

BATHROOMS: 2

WIDTH: 53'-5" **DEPTH:** 65'-10"

ENTER THIS BEAUTIFUL HOME through graceful archways and columns. The foyer, dining room and living room are one open space, defined by a creative room arrangement. The living room opens to the breakfast room and porch. The bedrooms are off a small hall reached through an archway. Two family bedrooms share a bath, while the master bedroom enjoys a private bath with a double-bowl vanity. A garage with storage and a utility room complete the floor plan. Please specify slab or crawlspace foundation when ordering.

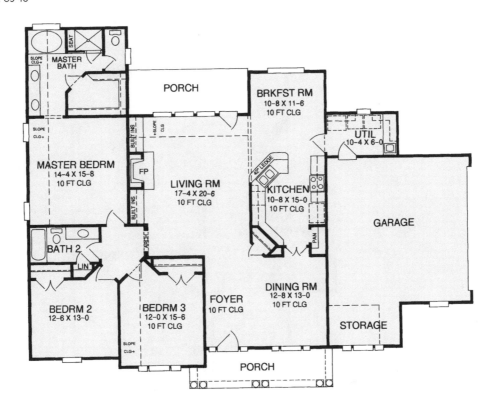

Sun-loving homes for entertaining

DESIGN HPT740174

SQUARE FOOTAGE: 1,707

BEDROOMS: 3

BATHROOMS: 2

WIDTH: 56'-6" DEPTH: 45'-8"

HERE'S A SENSATIONAL Mediterranean cottage that's well-suited for a coastal environment—yet it's ready for any place on earth. The covered front porch and arch-top windows lend great curb appeal and complement a spacious rear deck. An open formal dining room provides a place for memorable events. A coffered ceiling highlights the great room, anchored by a massive fireplace. Triple-window views enhance the rear of the plan and bring in natural light to the great room, breakfast area and master suite. To the front of the plan, two secondary bedrooms cluster around a full bath.

DECK

GREAT RM.
17-0 x 18-0

fireplace

shelves

BRKFST.
11-0 x 8-0

KIT.
11-0 x 10-0

MASTER BED RM.
13-8 x 15-0

walk-in closet

lin.

master bath

UTIL.
5-8 x 6-4
d w

BED RM./STUDY
11-0 x 12-0

bath

FOYER
5-8 x 14-4

DINING
11-0 x 13-0

GARAGE
21-0 x 21-0

cl

cl

cl

BED RM.
11-0 x 12-0

PORCH

DESIGN HPT740175

SQUARE FOOTAGE: 1,831

BEDROOMS: 3

BATHROOMS: 2

WIDTH: 54'-6" DEPTH: 60'-6"

THIS ONE-STORY, three-bedroom design takes its inspiration from the French and Neo-French Eclectic periods with the steeply pitched, hipped roof and the entry's elevated arch. Very modern in design, the interior boasts an efficient arrangement of private and social areas. The hub of social activities is definitely the great room, which adjoins the dining room and opens to the rear porch while enjoying a pass-through to the kitchen. Tray ceilings grace the formal dining room and the master suite, which includes two walk-in closets, double-sink vanity, tub and compartmented shower and toilet.

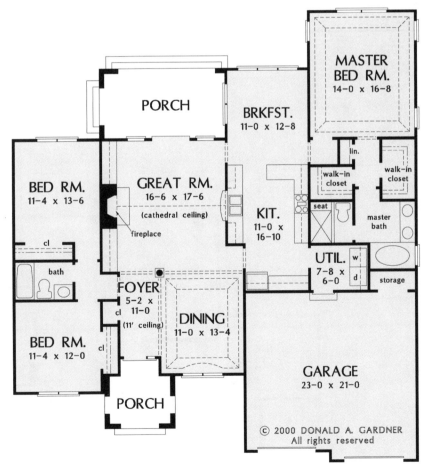

Sun-loving homes for entertaining

DESIGN HPT740176

SQUARE FOOTAGE: 1,712

BEDROOMS: 3

BATHROOMS: 2½

WIDTH: 67'-0" DEPTH: 42'-4"

A STYLISH STUCCO EXTERIOR enhances this home's curb appeal. A sunken great room offers a corner fireplace flanked by wide patio doors. A well-designed kitchen features an ideal view of the great room and fireplace through the breakfast-bar opening. The rear patio offers plenty of outdoor entertaining and relaxing space. The master suite features a private bath and walk-in closet. The master bath contains dual vanities, while the two family bedrooms each access a bath. A spacious two-car garage completes this plan.

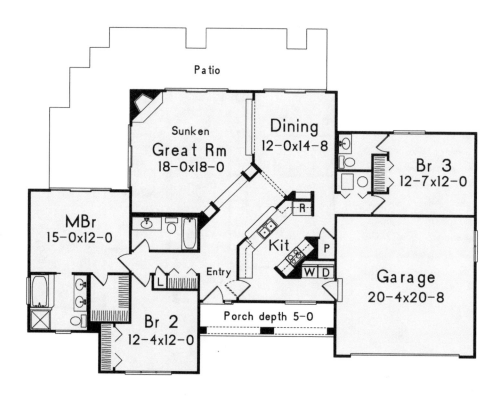

Patio

Sunken
Great Rm
18-0x18-0

Dining
12-0x14-8

Br 3
12-7x12-0

MBr
15-0x12-0

R

Kit

P

Entry

L

W D

Garage
20-4x20-8

Br 2
12-4x12-0

Porch depth 5-0

DESIGN HPT740177

SQUARE FOOTAGE: 2,098

BEDROOMS: 3

BATHROOMS: 2

WIDTH: 60'-0" DEPTH: 63'-8"

THIS THREE-BEDROOM home fits nicely into any neighborhood with its complex hipped roof and stucco facade offering a European/Mediterranean flair. The vaulted great room, with fireplace, built-ins and a window wall that opens to the covered porch, adjoins the elegant dining room where decorative columns and a tray ceiling set a formal tone. The rear porch can also be accessed as well by the master bedroom and the breakfast nook, which enjoys a sunny location abutting the kitchen.

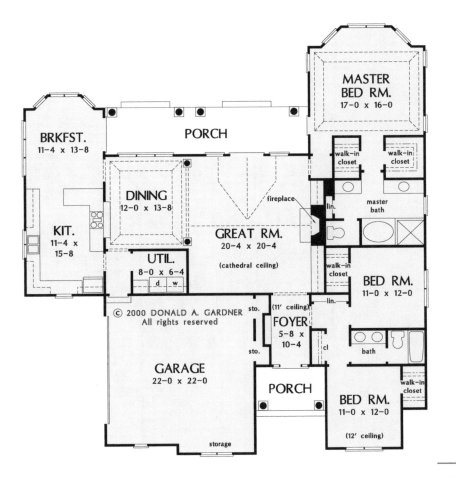

Sun-loving homes for entertaining

DESIGN HPT740178

SQUARE FOOTAGE: 2,367
BEDROOMS: 3
BATHROOMS: 2
WIDTH: 76'-0" DEPTH: 71'-4"

THE IMPRESSIVE ENTRY into this Mediterranean-style home leads directly into a spacious gathering room, with unique angles and a mitered glass window. This is the perfect home for the family that entertains! The large gathering room and covered porch with summer kitchen, are ready for a pool party! Elegance and style grace this split floor plan, with large bedrooms and a very spacious kitchen/breakfast nook area. The kitchen includes a center island and a walk-in pantry. The master suite showcases a fireplace next to French doors, which lead onto the covered porch at the rear, sweetly arranged for romantic evenings.

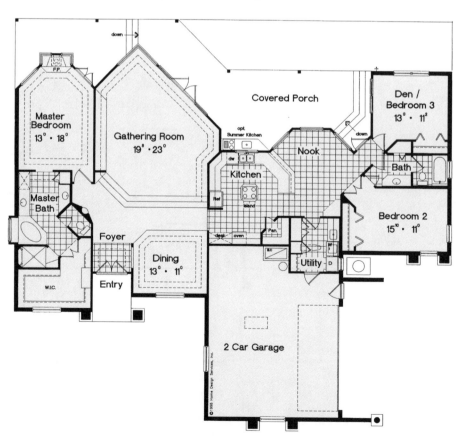

DESIGN HPT740179

SQUARE FOOTAGE: 2,551

BONUS SPACE: 287 square feet

BEDROOMS: 3

BATHROOMS: 3

WIDTH: 69'-8" DEPTH: 71'-4"

SHUTTERS AND MULTI-PANE windows dress up the exterior of this lovely stucco home. Formal and informal areas flow easily, beginning with the dining room sized to accommodate large parties and function with the adjacent living room. A gourmet kitchen is complete with a walk-in pantry and a cozy breakfast nook. Double doors lead to the spacious master suite. The lavish master bath features His and Hers walk-in closets, a tub framed by a columned archway, and an oversized shower. Off the angular hallway, two bedrooms share a Pullman-style bath and a study desk. A bonus room over the garage provides additional space.

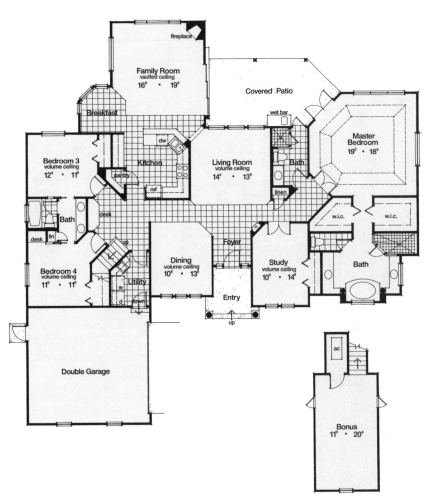

DESIGN HPT740180

SQUARE FOOTAGE: 2,300

FINISHED BASEMENT: 1,114 square feet

BEDROOMS: 3

BATHROOMS: 2

WIDTH: 56'-0" **DEPTH:** 61'-6"

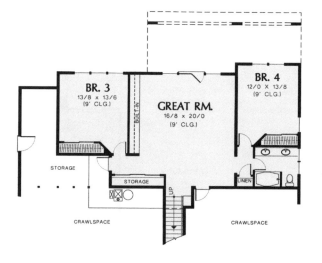

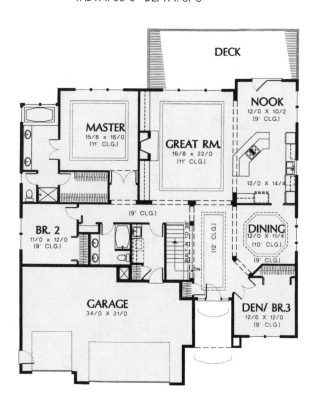

LOOKING FOR ALL THE WORLD like a one-story plan, this elegant hillside design has a surprise on the lower level. The main level is reached through an arched, recessed entry that opens to a twelve-foot ceiling. The formal dining room is on the right, next to a cozy den or Bedroom 3. Columns decorate the hall and separate it from the dining room and great room, which contains a tray ceiling and a fireplace flanked by built-ins. The breakfast nook and kitchen are just steps away, on the left. Lower-level space includes another great room with built-ins and two family bedrooms sharing a full bath.

DESIGN HPT740181

TOTAL: 5,878 square feet

FIRST FLOOR: 5,152 square feet

SECOND FLOOR: 726 square feet

BEDROOMS: 4

BATHROOMS: 5½

WIDTH: 146'-7"   DEPTH: 106'-7"

FROM THE MASTER bedroom suite to the detached four-car garage, this design will delight even the most discerning palates. While the formal living and dining rooms bid greeting as you enter, the impressive great room, with its cathedral ceiling, raised-hearth fireplace and veranda access, will take your breath away. A gallery hall leads to the kitchen and the family sleeping wing on the right and to the study, guest suite and master suite on the left. The large island kitchen, with its sunny breakfast nook, will be a gourmet's delight. The master suite includes a bayed sitting area, a dual fireplace shared with the study, and a luxurious bath. Each additional bedroom features its own bath and sitting area. Upstairs is a massive recreation room with a sunlit studio area and a bridge leading to an attic over the garage.

Rustic retreats for everyone

DESIGN HPT740182

TOTAL: 2,756 square feet

FIRST FLOOR: 1,855 square feet

SECOND FLOOR: 901 square feet

BEDROOMS: 3

BATHROOMS: 3½

WIDTH: 66'-0" DEPTH: 50'-0"

THIS SOUTHERN TIDEWATER COTTAGE is the perfect vacation hideaway. An octagonal great room with a multi-faceted vaulted ceiling illuminates the interior. The island kitchen is brightened by a bumped-out window and a pass-through to the lanai. Two walk-in closets and a whirlpool bath await to indulge the homeowner in the master suite. A set of double doors opens to the vaulted master lanai for quiet comfort. The U-shaped staircase leads to a loft, which overlooks the great room and the foyer. Two additional family bedrooms are offered with private baths. A computer center and a morning kitchen complete the upstairs.

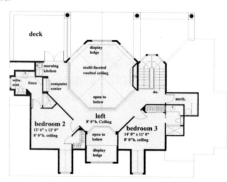

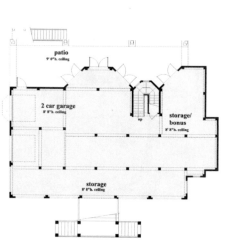

DESIGN HPT740183

TOTAL: 3,098 square feet

FIRST FLOOR: 2,146 square feet

SECOND FLOOR: 952 square feet

FINISHED BASEMENT: 187 square feet

BEDROOMS: 3

BATHROOMS: 3½

WIDTH: 52'-0" DEPTH: 65'-4"

OUTDOOR SPACES such as the inviting wraparound porch and the rear veranda expand the living area of this cottage. French doors, a fireplace and built-in cabinets adorn the great room. A private hall leads to the first-floor master suite. The upper level boasts a catwalk that overlooks the great room and the foyer. A secluded master wing enjoys a bumped-out window, a stunning tray ceiling and two walk-in closets. The island kitchen conveniently accesses the nook, dining area and the wet bar.

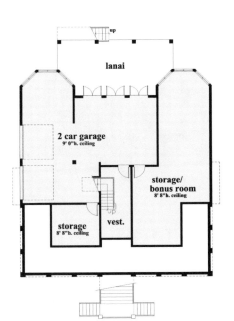

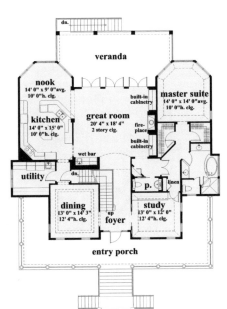

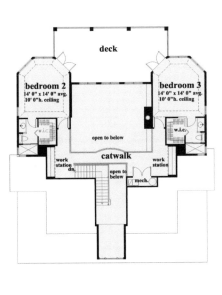

Rustic retreats for everyone

191

DESIGN HPT740184

TOTAL: 1,853 square feet

FIRST FLOOR: 1,342 square feet

SECOND FLOOR: 511 square feet

BEDROOMS: 3

BATHROOMS: 2

WIDTH: 44'-0" **DEPTH:** 40'-0"

AMENITIES ABOUND in this delightful two-story home. The foyer opens directly into the fantastic grand room, which offers a warming fireplace and two sets of double doors to the rear deck. The dining room also accesses this deck and a second deck shared with Bedroom 2. A convenient kitchen and another bedroom also reside on this level. Upstairs, the master bedroom reigns supreme. Entered through double doors, it pampers with a luxurious bath, walk-in closet, morning kitchen and private observation deck. This home is designed with a pier foundation.

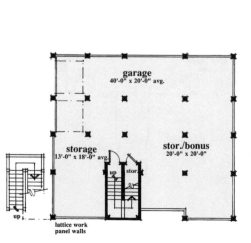

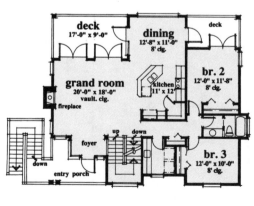

DESIGN HPT740185

TOTAL: 4,496 square feet

FIRST FLOOR: 3,294 square feet

SECOND FLOOR: 1,202 square feet

FINISHED BASEMENT: 1,366 square feet

BEDROOMS: 4

BATHROOMS: 4

WIDTH: 63'-0" DEPTH: 82'-0"

SUITED FOR A GOLF RESORT or lakeview site, this two-story, five-bedroom home includes room for plenty of guests. French doors open from the large front porch to the foyer, dining room and a family bedroom. French doors also lead from the hearth-warmed living room to the rear porch. The island kitchen features a breakfast area, walk-in pantry and convenient butler's pantry near the dining room. The master suite enjoys many luxuries, including private access to the rear porch. The second floor contains a family bedroom, media room with a balcony, a private study and two full baths. A kitchen, family bedroom, game room and plenty of extra storage adjoin a three-car garage in the walkout basement.

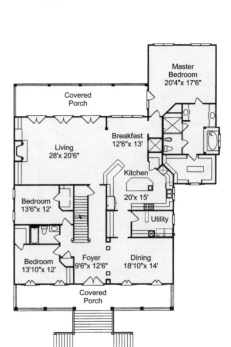

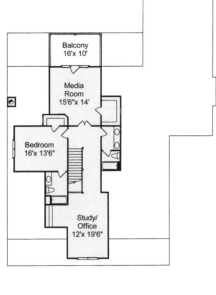

Rustic retreats for everyone

DESIGN HPT740186

TOTAL: 1,471 square feet

FIRST FLOOR: 895 square feet

SECOND FLOOR: 576 square feet

BEDROOMS: 3

BATHROOMS: 2

WIDTH: 26'-0" **DEPTH:** 36'-0"

HERE'S A FAVORITE waterfront home with plenty of space to kick back and relax. A lovely sun room opens from the dining room and allows great views. An angled hearth warms the living and dining areas. Three lovely windows brighten the dining space, which leads out to a stunning sun porch. The gourmet kitchen has an island counter with a snack bar. The first-floor master bedroom enjoys a walk-in closet and a nearby bath. Upstairs, a spacious bath with a whirlpool tub is thoughtfully placed between two bedrooms. A daylight basement allows a lower-level portico.

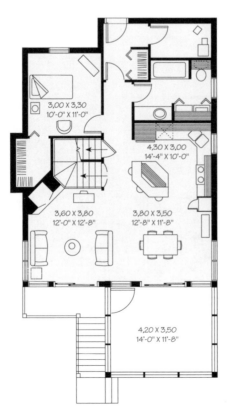

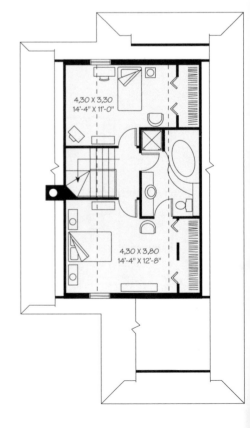

DESIGN HPT740187

TOTAL: 1,471 square feet

FIRST FLOOR: 895 square feet

SECOND FLOOR: 576 square feet

BEDROOMS: 3

BATHROOMS: 2

WIDTH: 26'-0" **DEPTH:** 36'-0"

THIS VACATION HOME enjoys a screened porch and sits on stilts to avoid any water damage. Truly a free-flowing plan, the dining room, living room and kitchen share a common space, with no walls separating them. An island snack counter in the kitchen provides plenty of space for food preparation. A family bedroom and full bath complete the first level. Upstairs, two additional bedrooms—with ample closet space—share a lavish bath, which includes a whirlpool tub and separate shower. This home is designed with a basement foundation.

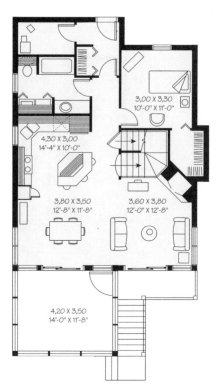

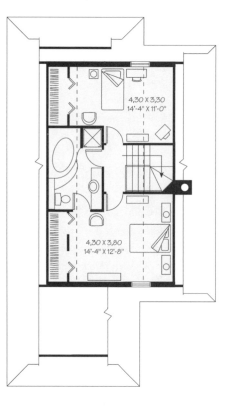

Rustic retreats for everyone

DESIGN HPT740188

TOTAL: 2,020 square feet

FIRST FLOOR: 1,182 square feet

SECOND FLOOR: 838 square feet

BEDROOMS: 4

BATHROOMS: 3

WIDTH: 34'-0" DEPTH: 52'-0"

THIS TWO-STORY coastal home finds its inspiration in a Craftsman style that's highlighted by ornamented gables. Open planning is the key with the living and dining areas sharing the front of the first floor with the U-shaped kitchen and stairway. Both the dining room and the living room access the second porch. The master suite boasts a walk-in closet, private vanity and angled tub. The utility room is efficiently placed between the kitchen and bath. Bedrooms 2 and 3 share a bath while Bedroom 4 enjoys a private bath.

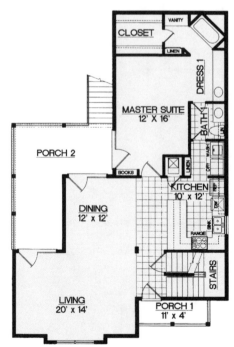

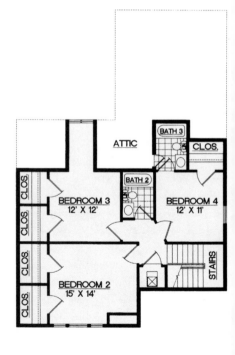

DESIGN HPT740189

TOTAL: 1,589 square feet

FIRST FLOOR: 617 square feet

SECOND FLOOR: 972 square feet

BONUS SPACE: 332 square feet

BEDROOMS: 3

BATHROOMS: 2

WIDTH: 36'-0" DEPTH: 30'-0"

THIS UNIQUE HOME BOASTS shutters, a siding exterior, stone detailing and an attractive front-facing balcony. Two family bedrooms and a full bath reside on the first floor. The second floor is home to the kitchen, dining room and hearth-warmed family room, which all flow into each other smoothly. The second-floor master bedroom enjoys a walk-through closet and private bath. The third floor is open for future expansion—more family bedrooms, a playroom or a rec room. This home is designed with a basement foundation.

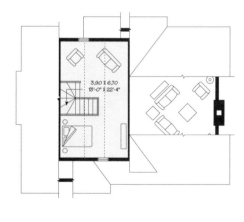

Rustic retreats for everyone

DESIGN HPT740190

TOTAL: 896 square feet

FIRST FLOOR: 448 square feet

SECOND FLOOR: 448 square feet

BEDROOMS: 2

BATHROOMS: 1½

WIDTH: 16'-0"   DEPTH: 41'-6"

PERFECT FOR A LAKESIDE, vacation or starter home, this two-story design is sure to be a favorite. A large railed porch on the first floor and the covered balcony on the second floor are available for watching the sunrise. On the first floor, the spacious living room is convenient to the kitchen and dining area. A powder room finishes off this level. Upstairs, the sleeping zone consists of two bedrooms, each with roomy closets, and a full hall bath with a linen closet. The front bedroom accesses the balcony.

DESIGN HPT740191

TOTAL: 2,228 square feet

FIRST FLOOR: 1,170 square feet

SECOND FLOOR: 1,058 square feet

BEDROOMS: 4

BATHROOMS: 2½

WIDTH: 30'-0" DEPTH: 51'-0"

AN ELEVATED PIER foundation, narrow width, and front and rear porches make this home perfect for waterfront lots, while its squared-off design makes it easy to afford. The great room, kitchen and breakfast area are all open for a casual and spacious feeling. Numerous windows enhance the area's volume. Flexible rooms located at the front of the home include a formal living or dining room and a study or bedroom with optional entry to the powder room. Upstairs, every bedroom (plus the master bath) enjoys porch access. The master suite features a tray ceiling, dual closets and a sizable bath with linen cabinets.

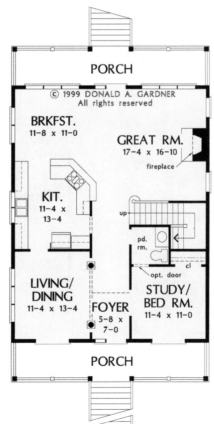

PORCH

BRKFST.
11-8 x 11-0

GREAT RM.
17-4 x 16-10
fireplace

KIT.
11-4 x 13-4

up

pd. rm.

cl

opt. door

LIVING/ DINING
11-4 x 13-4

FOYER
5-8 x 7-0

STUDY/ BED RM.
11-4 x 11-0

PORCH

PORCH

MASTER BED RM.
13-8 x 17-0

BED RM.
12-8 x 11-8

cl

lin.

bath

cl

walk-in closet

railing

down

UTIL.
d   w

master bath

lin.

lin.

foyer below

BED RM.
11-4 x 11-0

cl

PORCH

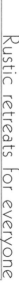

Rustic retreats for everyone

DESIGN HPT740192

TOTAL: 2,612 square feet

FIRST FLOOR: 1,500 square feet

SECOND FLOOR: 1,112 square feet

BEDROOMS: 4

BATHROOMS: 3

WIDTH: 42'-0" DEPTH: 49'-6"

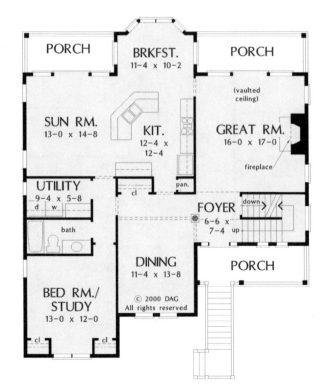

PORCHES FRONT AND BACK, a multitude of windows, and a narrow facade make this elevated pier foundation perfect for beach property or any waterfront lot. The main living areas are positioned at the rear of the home for the best views of the water. The great room features a vaulted ceiling, fireplace, and back porch access. The kitchen is open, sharing space with a bayed breakfast area and lovely sun room. The first floor includes a bedroom/study and full bath, while the master suite and two more family bedrooms can be found upstairs. The master suite boasts a private porch and sitting room with bay window.

DESIGN HPT740193

SQUARE FOOTAGE: 2,413

BEDROOMS: 3

BATHROOMS: 3

WIDTH: 66'-4" DEPTH: 62'-10"

AN IMPRESSIVE HIPPED ROOF and unique, turret-style roofs top the two front bedrooms of this extraordinary coastal home. An arched window in an eyebrow dormer crowns the double-door front entrance. A remarkable foyer creates quite a first impression and leads to the generous great room via a distinctive gallery with columns and a tray ceiling. The great room, master bedroom and master bath also boast tray ceilings—as well as numerous windows and back-porch access. The master bedroom not only provides a substantial amount of space in the walk-in closet, but also features a garden tub and massive shower. A delightful breakfast area and bay window complement the kitchen.

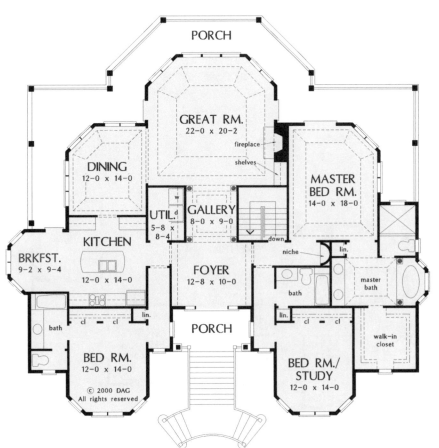

PORCH

GREAT RM.
22-0 x 20-2

fireplace

shelves

DINING
12-0 x 14-0

MASTER
BED RM.
14-0 x 18-0

UTIL.
5-8 x
8-4

GALLERY
8-0 x 9-0

KITCHEN
12-0 x 14-0

BRKFST.
9-2 x 9-4

niche

lin.

master
bath

FOYER
12-8 x 10-0

bath

bath

cl — cl

lin.

walk-in
closet

BED RM.
12-0 x 14-0

PORCH

BED RM./
STUDY
12-0 x 14-0

cl — cl

lin.

Rustic retreats for everyone

© 1999 Donald A Gardner, Inc.

DESIGN HPT740194

TOTAL: 2,380 square feet

FIRST FLOOR: 1,065 square feet

SECOND FLOOR: 1,019 square feet

LOFT: 296 square feet

BEDROOMS: 3

BATHROOMS: 3

WIDTH: 56'-10" DEPTH: 33'-7"

TAKING ADVANTAGE OF ITS BEAUTIFUL waterfront views, this coastal home features numerous windows and three porches. Clapboard siding, metal roofs and an elevated pier foundation grace the exterior for a traditional beach-house appearance. An open floor plan distinguishes the first floor, where the great room boasts a ventless fireplace and flanking built-ins. The kitchen is spacious yet efficient, with a helpful pantry. Upstairs, a sitting room with access to a third-story loft provides privacy for the master suite and a secondary bedroom. The master suite enjoys a luxurious bath, a generous walk-in closet, a wall of windows and a private screened porch.

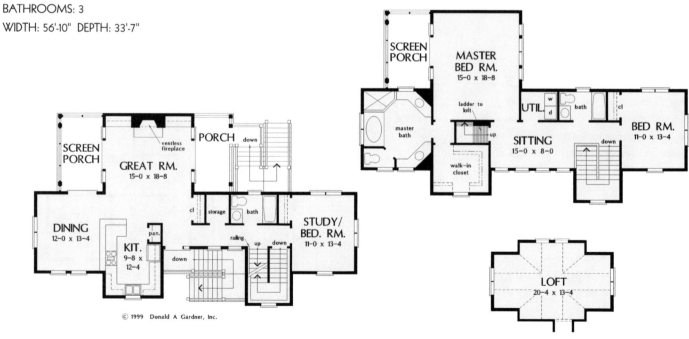

© 1999 Donald A Gardner, Inc.

MULTIPLE GABLES,

MULTIPLE GABLES, a center dormer with arched clerestory window, and a striking front staircase create visual excitement for this three-bedroom coastal home. Vaulted ceilings in the foyer and great room highlight a dramatic second-floor balcony that connects the two upstairs bedrooms, each with its own bath and private porch. The great room is generously proportioned with built-ins on either side of the fireplace. Private back porches enhance the dining room and the master suite, which boasts his and her walk-in closets and a magnificent bath with dual vanities, a garden tub, and separate shower.

DESIGN HPT740195

TOTAL: 2,390 square feet

FIRST FLOOR: 1,620 square feet

SECOND FLOOR: 770 square feet

BEDROOMS: 3

BATHROOMS: 3½

WIDTH: 49'-0" DEPTH: 58'-8"

Rustic retreats for everyone

DESIGN HPT740196

TOTAL: 1,037 square feet

FIRST FLOOR: 605 square feet

SECOND FLOOR: 432 square feet

BEDROOMS: 2

BATHROOMS: 1½

WIDTH: 33'-9" **DEPTH:** 27'-6"

A SHED-DORMERED ROOF with rolled eaves, a great stone chimney and a shingled exterior lend rusticity to this Craftsman-inspired retreat. Multi-wooden posts are anchored by stone piers, framing the welcoming front entry. Inside, a stone fireplace warms the living room, providing an ideal setting to curl up with a good book and enjoy the window seat that graces the bay window overlooking the front yard. A countertop separates the kitchen from the dining area, where sliding glass doors lead onto a rear patio. The second floor contains two bedrooms and a full bath. One of the bedrooms features a trio of period-style windows set into a centered dormer.

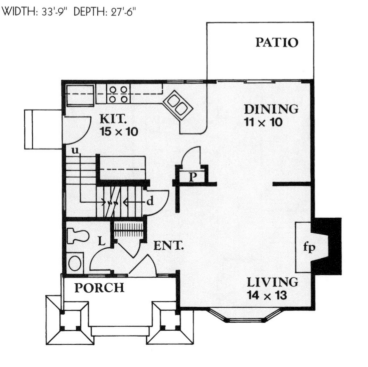

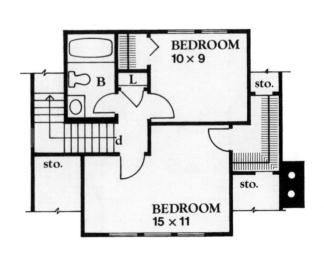

DESIGN HPT740197

SQUARE FOOTAGE: 1,404

BONUS SPACE: 256 square feet

BEDROOMS: 2

BATHROOMS: 2

WIDTH: 54'-7" DEPTH: 46'-6"

THIS RUSTIC CRAFTSMAN-STYLE COTTAGE provides an open interior with good flow to the outdoors. The front covered porch invites casual gatherings, while inside, the dining area is set for both everyday and planned occasions. Meal preparations are a breeze with a cooktop/snack-bar island in the kitchen. A centered fireplace in the great room shares its warmth with the dining room. A rear hall leads to the master bedroom and a secondary bedroom, while upstairs, a loft has space for computers.

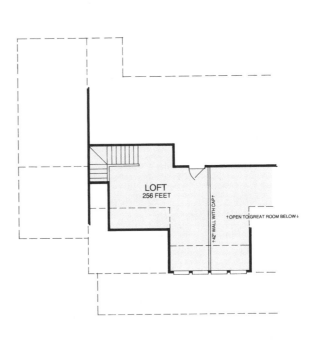

Rustic retreats for everyone

DESIGN HPT740198

SQUARE FOOTAGE: 1,792

BONUS SPACE: 494 square feet

BEDROOMS: 3

BATHROOMS: 2½

WIDTH: 63'-3" DEPTH: 52'-0"

A TOUCH OF RANCH and country flavor bring out the hometown goodness of this design. A porch leads to the foyer, which has a half bath and coat closet. Ahead is the great room with a fireplace and rear porch access through French doors. The dining room neighbors both the great room and the efficient kitchen. The breakfast bay is surrounded by windows and has a nice view of the rear porch. The master suite and two secondary bedrooms round out the first floor. Upstairs, bonus space is ideal for a growing family or just to spread out more.

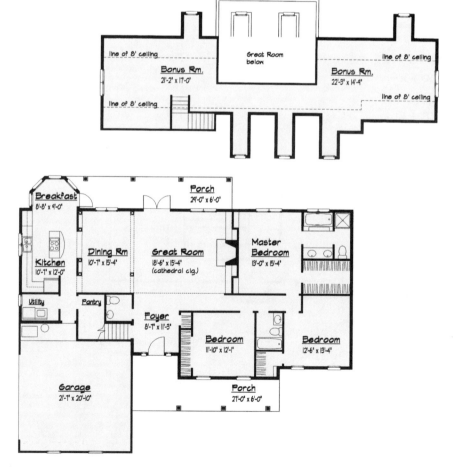

DESIGN HPT740199

SQUARE FOOTAGE: 1,501

BEDROOMS: 3

BATHROOMS: 2

WIDTH: 48'-0" DEPTH: 66'-0"

QUAINT AND PLEASING, this ideal design offers versatility. The covered porch provides homeowners with the opportunity to take pleasure in the rising sun or the starry night. Inside, the family room features a fireplace and is open to the kitchen and dining area. The master bedroom includes its own walk-in closet, a private bath and access to the rear covered porch. Two family bedrooms share a full hall bath and a hall linen closet. The two car-garage entry is located in the utility room.

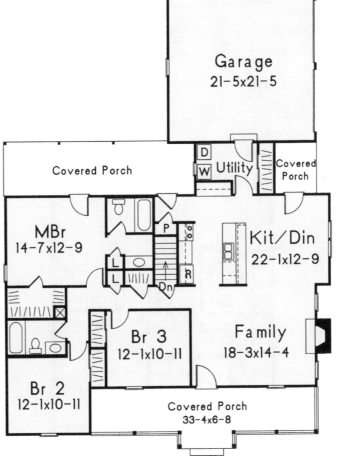

Garage
21-5x21-5

Covered Porch

D
W Utility Covered Porch

MBr
14-7x12-9

P

Kit/Din
22-1x12-9

L
L

Dn

R

Family
18-3x14-4

Br 3
12-1x10-11

Br 2
12-1x10-11

Covered Porch
33-4x6-8

Rustic retreats for everyone

DESIGN HPT740200

TOTAL: 1,605 square feet

FIRST FLOOR: 922 square feet

SECOND FLOOR: 683 square feet

BEDROOMS: 3

BATHROOMS: 2

WIDTH: 27'-7" DEPTH: 39'-5"

THIS CHARMING COTTAGE is the perfect size and configuration for a leisure-time home. A weather-protected entry opens to a mudroom and serves as a storage space and air-lock. The gathering area is comprised of a living room and a dining room and is warmed by a wood-burning stove. An entire wall of glass with sliding doors opens to a rear deck. The master bedroom is on the first floor and features a main-floor bath with an attached sauna. Two bedrooms and a full bath are on the second floor. Bedroom 2 has a private balcony.

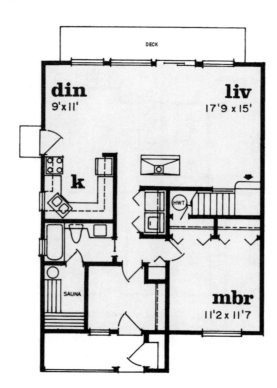

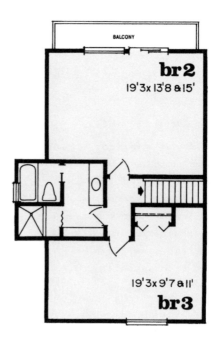

DESIGN HPT740201

TOTAL: 1,795 square feet

FIRST FLOOR: 1,157 square feet

SECOND FLOOR: 638 square feet

BEDROOMS: 3

BATHROOMS: 2½

WIDTH: 36'-0" DEPTH: 40'-0"

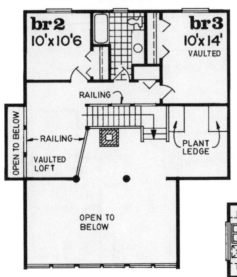

br2 10'x10'6

br3 10'x14' VAULTED

RAILING

OPEN TO BELOW

RAILING

VAULTED LOFT

PLANT LEDGE

OPEN TO BELOW

mbr 12'x14'2

DECK

SH.

k 13'7x11'

BENCH

FOYER

COUNTER

WOOD COLUMNS

din 8'x13' VAULTED

VAULTED

15'x17'8 **liv**

SUNKEN SPA

DECK

THIS LEISURE HOME IS PERFECT for outdoor living, with French doors opening to a large sun deck and sunken spa. The open-beam, vaulted ceiling and high window wall provide views for the living and dining rooms, which are decorated with wood columns and warmed by a fireplace. The step-saving U-shaped kitchen has ample counter space and a bar counter to the dining room. The master suite on the first floor features a walk-in closet and a private bath. A convenient mudroom with an adjoining laundry room accesses a rear deck. Two bedrooms on the second floor share a full bath.

Rustic retreats for everyone

DESIGN HPT740202

TOTAL: 1,607 square feet

FIRST FLOOR: 1,027 square feet

SECOND FLOOR: 580 square feet

BEDROOMS: 3

BATHROOMS: 2

WIDTH: 37'-4"   DEPTH: 44'-8"

THIS ECONOMICAL AND RUSTIC three-bedroom plan sports a relaxing country image with both front and back covered porches—a perfect mountain escape! The openness of the great room to the kitchen/dining areas and the loft/study area is reinforced with a shared cathedral ceiling. An abundance of windows in the great room, sliding glass doors in the kitchen and an over-the-sink window fill this open space with natural light and usher in the beauty of the outdoors. The first floor allows for two bedrooms, a full bath and a utility area. The master suite on the second floor has a walk-in closet and a private bath. Completing the second floor, a loft/study overlooks the great room below, providing space for quiet, reflective moments.

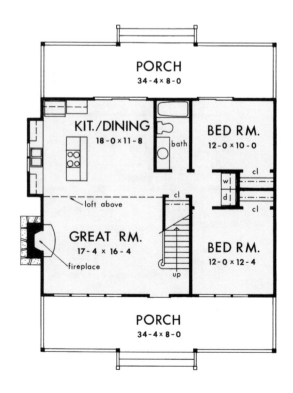

Quote One®

Cost to build? See page 214
to order complete cost estimate
to build this house in your area!

DESIGN HPT740203

TOTAL: 1,684 square feet

FIRST FLOOR: 1,100 square feet

SECOND FLOOR: 584 square feet

BEDROOMS: 3

BATHROOMS: 2

WIDTH: 36'-8" **DEPTH:** 45'-0"

A RELAXING COUNTRY IMAGE projects from the front and rear covered porches of this rustic three-bedroom home. Open planning extends to the great room, the dining room and the efficient kitchen. A shared cathedral ceiling creates an impressive space. Completing the first floor are two family bedrooms, a full bath and a handy utility area. The second floor contains the master suite featuring a spacious walk-in closet and a private bath with a whirlpool tub and separate corner shower. A generous loft/study overlooks the great room below.

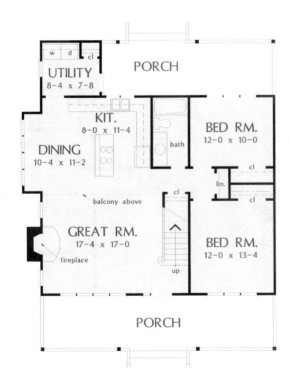

Quote One®

Cost to build? See page 214 to order complete cost estimate to build this house in your area!

Rustic retreats for everyone

© 1991 Donald A. Gardner Architects, Inc.

A MOUNTAIN RETREAT, this rustic home features covered porches at the front and rear. Enjoy open living in the great room and kitchen/dining room combination. Here, a fireplace provides the focal point and a warm welcome that continues into the L-shaped island kitchen. A cathedral ceiling graces the great room and gives an open, inviting sense of space. Two bedrooms—one with a walk-in closet—and a full bath on the first level are complemented by a master bedroom on the second floor. This suite includes a walk-in closet and deluxe bath. Attic storage is available on the second floor.

DESIGN HPT740204

TOTAL: 1,338 square feet
FIRST FLOOR: 1,002 square feet
SECOND FLOOR: 336 square feet
BEDROOMS: 3
BATHROOMS: 2
WIDTH: 36'-8" DEPTH: 44'-8"

©1991 Donald A. Gardner Architects, Inc.

PORCH
33-8 x 8-0

**KIT./
DINING**
16-8 x 10-4

walk-in
closet

BED RM.
11-4 x 10-0

w   d

balcony above

bath

(cathedral ceiling)

cl

GREAT RM.
17-4 x 17-8

cl

fireplace

BED RM.
11-4 x 10-0

up

PORCH
33-8 x 8-0

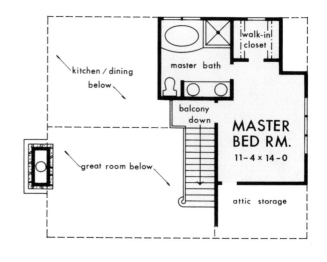

kitchen / dining
below

master bath

walk-in
closet

balcony
down

great room below

**MASTER
BED RM.**
11-4 x 14-0

attic storage

LET US SHOW YOU OUR HOME BLUEPRINT PACKAGE.

BUILDING A HOME? PLANNING A HOME?

OUR BLUEPRINT PACKAGE HAS NEARLY EVERYTHING YOU NEED TO GET THE JOB DONE RIGHT,

whether you're working on your own or with help from an architect, designer, builder or subcontractors. Each Blueprint Package is the result of many hours of work by licensed architects or professional designers.

QUALITY

Hundreds of hours of painstaking effort have gone into the development of your blueprint plan. Each home has been quality-checked by professionals to insure accuracy and buildability.

VALUE

Because we sell in volume, you can buy professional quality blueprints at a fraction of their development cost. With our plans, your dream home design costs substantially less than the fees charged by architects.

SERVICE

Once you've chosen your favorite home plan, you'll receive fast, efficient service whether you choose to mail or fax your order to us or call us toll free at 1-800-521-6797. After you have received your order, call for customer service toll free 1-888-690-1116.

SATISFACTION

Over 50 years of service to satisfied home plan buyers provide us unparalleled experience and knowledge in producing quality blueprints.

ORDER TOLL FREE 1-800-521-6797

After you've looked over our Blueprint Package and Important Extras, call toll free on our Blueprint Hotline: 1-800-521-6797, for current pricing and availability prior to mailing the order form on page 221. We're ready and eager to serve you. After you have received your order, call for customer service toll free 1-888-690-1116.

Each set of blueprints is an interrelated collection of detail sheets which includes components such as floor plans, interior and exterior elevations, dimensions, cross-sections, diagrams and notations. These sheets show exactly how your house is to be built.

SETS MAY INCLUDE:

FRONTAL SHEET

This artist's sketch of the exterior of the house gives you an idea of how the house will look when built and landscaped. Large floor plans show all levels of the house and provide an overview of your new home's livability, as well as a handy reference for deciding on furniture placement.

FOUNDATION PLANS

This sheet shows the foundation layout including support walls, excavated and unexcavated areas, if any, and foundation notes. If slab construction rather than basement, the plan shows footings and details for a monolithic slab. This page, or another in the set, may include a sample plot plan for locating your house on a building site.

DETAILED FLOOR PLANS

These plans show the layout of each floor of the house. Rooms and interior spaces are carefully dimensioned and keys are given for cross-section details provided later in the plans. The positions of electrical outlets and switches are shown.

HOUSE CROSS-SECTIONS

Large-scale views show sections or cut-aways of the foundation, interior walls, exterior walls, floors, stairways and roof details. Additional cross-sections may show important changes in floor, ceiling or roof heights or the relationship of one level to another. Extremely valuable for construction, these sections show exactly how the various parts of the house fit together.

INTERIOR ELEVATIONS

Many of our drawings show the design and placement of kitchen and bathroom cabinets, laundry areas, fireplaces, bookcases and other built-ins. Little "extras," such as mantelpiece and wainscoting drawings, plus molding sections, provide details that give your home that custom touch.

EXTERIOR ELEVATIONS

These drawings show the front, rear and sides of your house and give necessary notes on exterior materials and finishes. Particular attention is given to cornice detail, brick and stone accents or other finish items that make your home unique.

INTRODUCING IMPORTANT PLANNING AND CONSTRUCTION AIDS DEVELOPED BY OUR PROFESSIONALS TO HELP YOU SUCCEED IN YOUR HOME-BUILDING PROJECT

MATERIALS LIST

(Note: Because of the diversity of local building codes, our Materials List does not include mechanical materials.)

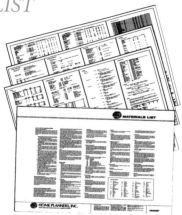

For many of the designs in our portfolio, we offer a customized materials take-off that is invaluable in planning and estimating the cost of your new home. This Materials List outlines the quantity, type and size of materials needed to build your house (with the exception of mechanical system items). Included are framing lumber, windows and doors, kitchen and bath cabinetry, rough and finish hardware, and much more. This handy list helps you or your builder cost out materials and serves as a reference sheet when you're compiling bids. Some Materials Lists may be ordered before blueprints are ordered, call for information.

SPECIFICATION OUTLINE

This valuable 16-page document is critical to building your house correctly. Designed to be filled in by you or your builder, this book lists 166 stages or items crucial to the building process. It provides a comprehensive review of the construction process and helps in choosing materials. When combined with the blueprints, a signed contract, and a schedule, it becomes a legal document and record for the building of your home.

QUOTE ONE®

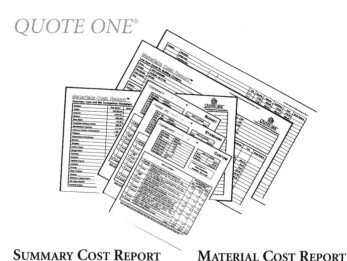

SUMMARY COST REPORT   **MATERIAL COST REPORT**

A product for estimating the cost of building select designs, the Quote One® system is available in two separate stages: The Summary Cost Report and the Material Cost Report.

The **Summary Cost Report** is the first stage in the package and shows the total cost per square foot for your chosen home in your zip-code area and then breaks that cost down into various categories showing the costs for building materials, labor and installation. The report includes three grades: Budget, Standard and Custom. These reports allow you to evaluate your building budget and compare the costs of building a variety of homes in your area.

Make even more informed decisions about your home-building project with the second phase of our package, our **Material Cost Report.** This tool is invaluable in planning and estimating the cost of your new home. The material and installation (labor and equipment) cost is shown for each of over 1,000 line items provided in the Materials List (Standard grade), which is included when you purchase this estimating tool. It allows you to determine building costs for your specific zip-code area and for your chosen home design. Space is allowed for additional estimates from contractors and subcontractors, such as for mechanical materials, which are not included in our packages. This invaluable tool includes a Materials List. A Material Cost Report cannot be ordered before blueprints are ordered. Call for details. In addition, ask about our Home Planners Estimating Package.

If you are interested in a plan that is not indicated as Quote One®, please call and ask our sales reps. They will be happy to verify the status for you. To order these invaluable reports, use the order form.

CONSTRUCTION INFORMATION

If you want to know more about techniques—and deal more confidently with subcontractors — we offer these useful sheets. Each set is an excellent tool that will add to your understanding of these technical subjects. These helpful details provide general construction information and are not specific to any single plan.

PLUMBING

The Blueprint Package includes locations for all the plumbing fixtures, including sinks, lavatories, tubs, showers, toilets, laundry trays and water heaters. However, if you want to know more about the complete plumbing system, these Plumbing Details will prove very useful. Prepared to meet requirements of the National Plumbing Code, these fact-filled sheets give general information on pipe schedules, fittings, sump-pump details, water-softener hookups, septic system details and much more. Sheets also include a glossary of terms.

ELECTRICAL

The locations for every electrical switch, plug and outlet are shown in your Blueprint Package. However, these Electrical Details go further to take the mystery out of household electrical systems. Prepared to meet requirements of the National Electrical Code, these comprehensive drawings come packed with helpful information, including wire sizing, switch-installation schematics, cable-routing details, appliance wattage, doorbell hook-ups, typical service panel circuitry and much more. A glossary of terms is also included.

CONSTRUCTION

The Blueprint Package contains information an experienced builder needs to construct a particular house. However, it doesn't show all the ways that houses can be built, nor does it explain alternate construction methods. To help you understand how your house will be built—and offer additional techniques—this set of Construction Details depicts the materials and methods used to build foundations, fireplaces, walls, floors and roofs. Where appropriate, the drawings show acceptable alternatives.

MECHANICAL

These Mechanical Details contain fundamental principles and useful data that will help you make informed decisions and communicate with subcontractors about heating and cooling systems. Drawings contain instructions and samples that allow you to make simple load calculations, and preliminary sizing and costing analysis. Covered are the most commonly used systems from heat pumps to solar fuel systems. The package is filled with illustrations and diagrams to help you visualize components and how they relate to one another.

THE HANDS-ON HOME FURNITURE PLANNER

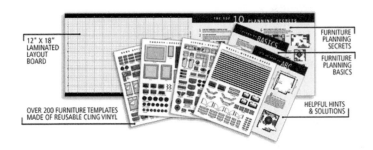

Effectively plan the space in your home using The **Hands-On Home Furniture Planner**. It's fun and easy—no more moving heavy pieces of furniture to see how the room will go together. And you can try different layouts, moving furniture at a whim.

The kit includes reusable peel and stick furniture templates that fit onto a 12" x 18" laminated layout board—space enough to layout every room in your home.

Also included in the package are a number of helpful planning tools. You'll receive:

- ✓ Helpful hints and solutions for difficult situations.
- ✓ Furniture planning basics to get you started.
- ✓ Furniture planning secrets that let you in on some of the tricks of professional designers.

The **Hands-On Home Furniture Planner** is the one tool that no new homeowner or home remodeler should be without. It's also a perfect housewarming gift!

To Order, Call Toll Free
1-800-521-6797

After you've looked over our Blueprint Package and Important Extras on these pages, call for current pricing and availability prior to mailing the order form. We're ready and eager to serve you. After you have received your order, call for customer service toll free 1-888-690-1116.

THE FINISHING TOUCHES...

THE DECK BLUEPRINT PACKAGE

Many of the homes in this book can be enhanced with a professionally designed Home Planners Deck Plan. Those homes marked with a **D** have a complementary Deck Plan, sold separately, which includes a Deck Plan Frontal Sheet, Deck Framing and Floor Plans, Deck Elevations and a Deck Materials List. A Standard Deck Details Package, also available, provides all the how-to information necessary for building *any* deck. Our Complete Deck Building Package contains one set of Custom Deck Plans of your choice, plus one set of Standard Deck Building Details, all for one low price. Our plans and details are carefully prepared in an easy-to-understand format that will guide you through every stage of your deck-building project. This page shows a sample Deck layout to match your favorite house. See Blueprint Price Schedule for ordering information.

THE LANDSCAPE BLUEPRINT PACKAGE

For the homes marked with an **L** in this book, Home Planners has created a front-yard Landscape Plan that is complementary in design to the house plan. These comprehensive blueprint packages include a Frontal Sheet, Plan View, Regionalized Plant & Materials List, a sheet on Planting and Maintaining Your Landscape, Zone Maps and Plant Size and Description Guide. These plans will help you achieve professional results, adding value and enjoyment to your property for years to come. Each set of blueprints is a full 18" x 24" in size with clear, complete instructions and easy-to-read type. A sample Landscape Plan is shown below. See Blueprint Price Schedule for ordering information.

CONTEMPORARY LEISURE DECK
Deck ODA021

CAPE COD COTTAGE
Landscape OLA003

REGIONAL ORDER MAP

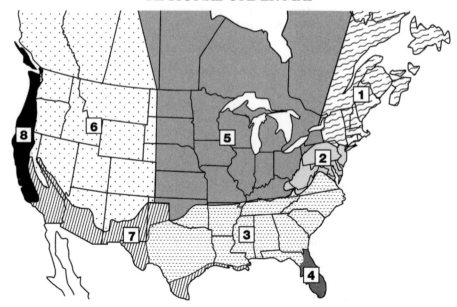

Most Landscape Plans are available with a Plant & Materials List adapted by horticultural experts to 8 different regions of the country. Please specify the Geographic Region when ordering your plan. See Blueprint Price Schedule for ordering information and regional availability.

Region	1	Northeast
Region	2	Mid-Atlantic
Region	3	Deep South
Region	4	Florida & Gulf Coast
Region	5	Midwest
Region	6	Rocky Mountains
Region	7	Southern California & Desert Southwest
Region	8	Northern California & Pacific Northwest

BLUEPRINT PRICE SCHEDULE

Prices guaranteed through December 31, 2003

TIERS	1-SET STUDY PACKAGE	4-SET BUILDING PACKAGE	8-SET BUILDING PACKAGE	1-SET REPRODUCIBLE*
P1	$20	$50	$90	$140
P2	$40	$70	$110	$160
P3	$70	$100	$140	$190
P4	$100	$130	$170	$220
P5	$140	$170	$210	$270
P6	$180	$210	$250	$310
A1	$440	$480	$520	$660
A2	$480	$520	$560	$720
A3	$530	$575	$615	$800
A4	$575	$620	$660	$870
C1	$620	$665	$710	$935
C2	$670	$715	$760	$1000
C3	$715	$760	$805	$1075
C4	$765	$810	$855	$1150
L1	$870	$925	$975	$1300
L2	$945	$1000	$1050	$1420
L3	$1050	$1105	$1155	$1575
L4	$1155	$1210	$1260	$1735
SQ1				.35/sq. ft.

* Requires a fax number

OPTIONS FOR PLANS IN TIERS A1–L4

Additional Identical Blueprints
in same order for "A1–L4" price plans ....$50 per set
Reverse Blueprints (mirror image)
with 4- or 8-set order for "A1–L4" plans.......................................$50 fee per order
Specification Outlines..$10 each
Materials Lists for "A1–C3" plans ....$60 each
Materials Lists for "C4–L4" plans..$70 each

OPTIONS FOR PLANS IN TIERS P1–P6

Additional Identical Blueprints
in same order for "P1–P6" price plans...$10 per set
Reverse Blueprints (mirror image) for "P1–P6" price plans ....$10 fee per order
1 Set of Deck Construction Details ....$14.95 each
Deck Construction Package ....**add $10 to Building Package price**
(includes 1 set of "P1–P6" plans, plus
1 set Standard Deck Construction Details)

IMPORTANT NOTES

SQ one-set building package includes one set of reproducible vellum
construction drawings plus one set of study blueprints.
The 1-set study package is marked "not for construction."
Prices for 4- or 8-set Building Packages honored only at time of original order.
Some foundations carry a $225 surcharge.
Right-reading reverse blueprints, if available, will incur a $165 surcharge.
Additional identical blueprints may be purchased within 60 days of original order.

TO USE THE INDEX,

refer to the design number listed in numerical order (a helpful page reference is also given). Note the price tier and refer to the Blueprint Price Schedule above for the cost of one, four or eight sets of blueprints or the cost of a reproducible drawing. Additional prices are shown for identical and reverse blueprint sets, as well as a very useful Materials List for some of the plans. Also note in the Plan Index those plans that have Deck Plans or Landscape Plans. Refer to the schedules above for prices of these plans. The letter "Y" identifies plans that are part of our Quote One® estimating service and those that offer Materials Lists.

TO ORDER,

Call toll free 1-800-521-6797 for current pricing and availability prior to mailing the order form. FAX: 1-800-224-6699 or 520-544-3086.

PLAN INDEX

DESIGN	PRICE	PAGE	MATERIALS LIST	QUOTE ONE®	DECK	DECK PRICE	LANDSCAPE	LANDSCAPE PRICE	REGIONS
HPT740001	C3	5							
HPT740002	C3	8	Y						
HPT740003	C3	11							
HPT740004	C3	12							
HPT740005	L1	13							
HPT740006	C1	14	Y						
HPT740007	C4	15							
HPT740008	C1	16						OLA001	P3	123568
HPT740009	A3	17							
HPT740010	A4	18	Y	Y					
HPT740011	C2	19							
HPT740012	L2	20							
HPT740013	C4	21							
HPT740014	C2	22	Y						
HPT740015	A4	23	Y	Y					
HPT740016	C3	24							

PLAN INDEX

DESIGN	PRICE	PAGE	MATERIALS LIST	QUOTE ONE®	DECK	DECK PRICE	LANDSCAPE	LANDSCAPE PRICE	REGIONS
HPT740017	L1	25	Y	Y					
HPT740018	L1	26	Y	Y					
HPT740019	A3	27	Y						
HPT740020	A4	28	Y						
HPT740021	C1	29	Y						
HPT740022	C3	30		Y					
HPT740023	C2	31							
HPT740024	C1	32							
HPT740025	C1	33	Y						
HPT740026	A3	34							
HPT740027	A4	35							
HPT740028	A4	36							
HPT740029	A2	37							
HPT740030	C2	38	Y						
HPT740031	C4	39							
HPT740032	C2	40							
HPT740033	C3	41							
HPT740034	C1	42							
HPT740035	C4	43							
HPT740036	C1	44							
HPT740037	C4	45		Y					
HPT740038	C1	46							
HPT740039	C2	47							
HPT740040	C4	48							
HPT740041	C2	49							
HPT740042	L1	50							
HPT740043	C1	51	Y						
HPT740044	C2	52							
HPT740045	C1	53	Y	Y					
HPT740046	C4	54							
HPT740047	C1	55							
HPT740048	C2	56							
HPT740049	A4	57	Y						
HPT740050	C1	58							
HPT740051	A4	59	Y						
HPT740052	C1	60							
HPT740053	C2	61							
HPT740054	C1	62	Y						
HPT740055	C3	63							
HPT740056	A3	64	Y						
HPT740057	C1	65	Y	Y					
HPT740058	C1	66	Y						
HPT740059	A3	67	Y						
HPT740060	A4	68	Y						
HPT740061	C1	69							
HPT740062	A3	70							
HPT740063	C2	71	Y	Y					
HPT740064	A4	72	Y						
HPT740065	A4	73	Y						
HPT740066	A2	74	Y						
HPT740067	C1	75	Y						
HPT740068	C2	76	Y						
HPT740069	A3	77	Y						
HPT740070	A4	78	Y						
HPT740071	C1	79							
HPT740072	A3	80	Y						
HPT740073	C2	81							
HPT740074	C1	82							
HPT740075	C3	83							
HPT740076	A4	84							
HPT740077	C2	85	Y	Y					
HPT740078	A3	86							
HPT740079	C1	87							
HPT740080	C3	88							
HPT740081	C2	89							
HPT740082	C2	90							
HPT740083	C1	91							
HPT740084	C3	92							
HPT740085	C3	93							
HPT740086	C1	94							
HPT740087	A4	95							
HPT740088	A3	96	Y						
HPT740089	L1	97							
HPT740090	L2	98							
HPT740091	C2	99							
HPT740092	C2	100							
HPT740093	L2	101							
HPT740094	A4	102	Y						
HPT740095	A3	103							
HPT740096	A4	104	Y						
HPT740097	A4	105	Y						
HPT740098	A3	106	Y						
HPT740099	A4	107	Y						
HPT740100	C2	108	Y						
HPT740101	C2	109	Y						
HPT740102	A4	110	Y						
HPT740103	A4	111	Y						
HPT740104	C3	112							
HPT740105	C1	113							
HPT740106	A3	114							
HPT740107	A4	115							
HPT740108	A4	116	Y	Y			OLA001	P3	123568
HPT740109	A4	117							
HPT740110	C2	118							

Before filling out

the order form,

please call us on

our Toll-Free

Blueprint Hotline

1-800-521-6797.

You may want to

learn more about

our services and

products. Here's

some information

you will find helpful.

OUR EXCHANGE POLICY

With the exception of reproducible plan orders, we will exchange your entire first order for an equal or greater number of blueprints within our plan collection within 90 days of the original order. The entire content of your original order must be returned before an exchange will be processed. Please call our customer service department for your return authorization number and shipping instructions. If the returned blueprints look used, redlined or copied, we will not honor your exchange. Fees for exchanging your blueprints are as follows: 20% of the amount of the original order...plus the difference in cost if exchanging for a design in a higher price bracket or less the difference in cost if exchanging for a design in a lower price bracket. **(Reproducible blueprints are not exchangeable or refundable.)** Please call for current postage and handling prices. Shipping and handling charges are not refundable.

ABOUT REPRODUCIBLES

When purchasing a reproducible you may be required to furnish a fax number. The designer will fax documents that you must sign and return to them before shipping will take place.

ABOUT REVERSE BLUEPRINTS

Although lettering and dimensions will appear backward, reverses will be a useful aid if you decide to flop the plan. See Price Schedule and Plans Index for pricing.

REVISING, MODIFYING AND CUSTOMIZING PLANS

Like many homeowners who buy these plans, you and your builder, architect or engineer may want to make changes to them. We recommend purchase of a reproducible plan for any changes made by your builder, licensed architect or engineer. As set forth below, we cannot assume any responsibility for blueprints which have been changed, whether by you, your builder or by professionals selected by you or referred to you by us, because such individuals are outside our supervision and control.

ARCHITECTURAL AND ENGINEERING SEALS

Some cities and states are now requiring that a licensed architect or engineer review and "seal" a blueprint, or officially approve it, prior to construction due to concerns over energy costs, safety and other factors. Prior to application for a building permit or the start of actual construction, we strongly advise that you consult your local building official who can tell you if such a review is required.

ABOUT THE DESIGNS

The architects and designers whose work appears in this publication are among America's leading residential designers. Each plan was designed to meet the requirements of a nationally recognized model building code in effect at the time and place the plan was drawn. Because national building codes change from time to time, plans may not comply with any such code at the time they are sold to a customer. In addition, building officials may not accept these plans as final construction documents of record as the plans may need to be modified and additional drawings and details added to suit local conditions and requirements. We strongly advise that purchasers consult a licensed architect or engineer, and their local building official, before starting any construction related to these plans.

LOCAL BUILDING CODES AND ZONING REQUIREMENTS

At the time of creation, our plans are drawn to specifications published by the Building Officials and Code Administrators (BOCA) International, Inc.; the Southern Building Code Congress (SBCCI) International, Inc.; the International Conference of Building Officials (ICBO); or the Council of American Building Officials (CABO). Our plans are designed to meet or exceed national building standards. Because of the great differences in geography and climate throughout the United States and Canada, each state, county and municipality has its own building codes, zone requirements, ordinances and building regulations. Your plan may need to be modified to comply with local requirements regarding snow loads, energy codes, soil and seismic conditions and a wide range of other matters. In addition, you may need to obtain permits or inspections from local governments before and in the course of construction. Prior to using blueprints ordered from us, we strongly advise that you consult a licensed architect or engineer—and speak with your local building official—before applying for any permit or beginning construction. We authorize the use of our blueprints on the express condition that you strictly comply with all local building codes, zoning requirements and other applicable laws, regulations, ordinances and requirements. Notice: Plans for homes to be built in Nevada must be re-drawn by a Nevada-registered professional. Consult your building official for more information on this subject.

Toll Free
1-800-521-6797

REGULAR OFFICE HOURS:
8:00 a.m.-9:00 p.m. EST, Monday-Friday

If we receive your order by 3:00 p.m. EST, Monday-Friday, we'll process it and ship within **two business days**. When ordering by phone, please have your credit card or check information ready. We'll also ask you for the Order Form Key Number at the bottom of the order form.

By FAX: Copy the Order Form on the next page and send it on our FAX line: 1-800-224-6699 or 520-544-3086.

Canadian Customers
Order Toll Free 1-877-223-6389

DISCLAIMER

The designers we work with have put substantial care and effort into the creation of their blueprints. However, because they cannot provide on-site consultation, supervision and control over actual construction, and because of the great variance in local building requirements, building practices and soil, seismic, weather and other conditions, WE CANNOT MAKE ANY WARRANTY, EXPRESS OR IMPLIED, WITH RESPECT TO THE CONTENT OR USE OF THE BLUEPRINTS, INCLUDING BUT NOT LIMITED TO ANY WARRANTY OF MERCHANTABILITY OR OF FITNESS FOR A PARTICULAR PURPOSE. ITEMS, PRICES, TERMS AND CONDITIONS ARE SUBJECT TO CHANGE WITHOUT NOTICE. REPRODUCIBLE PLAN ORDERS MAY REQUIRE A CUSTOMER'S SIGNED RELEASE BEFORE SHIPPING.

TERMS AND CONDITIONS

These designs are protected under the terms of United States Copyright Law and may not be copied or reproduced in any way, by any means, unless you have purchased Reproducibles which clearly indicate your right to copy or reproduce. We authorize the use of your chosen design as an aid in the construction of one single family home only. You may not use this design to build a second or multiple dwellings without purchasing another blueprint or blueprints or paying additional design fees.

HOW MANY BLUEPRINTS DO YOU NEED?

Although a standard building package may satisfy many states, cities and counties, some plans may require certain changes. For your convenience, we have developed a Reproducible plan which allows a local professional to modify and make up to 10 copies of your revised plan. As our plans are all copyright protected, with your purchase of the Reproducible, we will supply you with a Copyright release letter. The number of copies you may need: 1 for owner; 3 for builder; 2 for local building department and 1-3 sets for your mortgage lender.

ORDER TOLL FREE!

For information about any of our services or to order call 1-800-521-6797

Browse our website: www.eplans.com

BLUEPRINTS ARE NOT REFUNDABLE EXCHANGES ONLY

For Customer Service, call toll free 1-888-690-1116.

HOME PLANNERS, LLC wholly owned by Hanley-Wood, LLC
3275 WEST INA ROAD, SUITE 110 • TUCSON, ARIZONA • 85741

THE BASIC BLUEPRINT PACKAGE

Rush me the following (please refer to the Plans Index and Price Schedule in this section):

___Set(s) of reproducibles*, plan number(s) _____ $_____
  indicate foundation type _____ surcharge (if applicable): $_____
___Set(s) of blueprints, plan number(s) _____ indicate foundation type _____
  indicate foundation type _____ surcharge (if applicable): $_____
___Additional identical blueprints (standard or reverse) in same order @ $50 per set $_____
___Reverse blueprints @ $50 fee per order. Right-reading reverse @ $165 surcharge $_____

IMPORTANT EXTRAS

Rush me the following:

___Materials List: $60 (Must be purchased with Blueprint set.) Add $10 for Schedule C4–L4 plans $_____
___**Quote One**® Summary Cost Report @ $29.95 for one, $14.95 for each additional,
  for plans _____ $_____
  Building location: City _____ Zip Code _____
___**Quote One**® Material Cost Report @ $120 Schedules P1–C3; $130 Schedules C4–L4,
  for plan_____(Must be purchased with Blueprints set.) $_____
  Building location: City _____ Zip Code _____
___Specification Outlines @ $10 each $_____
___Detail Sets @ $14.95 each; any two $22.95; any three $29.95; all four for $39.95 (save $19.85) $_____
___❑ Plumbing ❑ Electrical ❑ Construction ❑ Mechanical
___Home Furniture Planner @ $15.95 each $_____

DECK BLUEPRINTS

(Please refer to the Plans Index and Price Schedule in this section)

___Set(s) of Deck Plan _____. $_____
___Additional identical blueprints in same order @ $10 per set. $_____
___Reverse blueprints @ $10 fee per order. $_____
___Set of Standard Deck Details @ $14.95 per set. $_____
___Set of Complete Deck Construction Package (Best Buy!) Add $10 to Building Package.
  Includes Custom Deck Plan _____ Plus Standard Deck Details

LANDSCAPE BLUEPRINTS

(Please refer to the Plans Index and Price Schedule in this section.)

___Set(s) of Landscape Plan _____ $_____
___Additional identical blueprints in same order @ $10 per set $_____
___Reverse blueprints @ $10 fee per order $_____

Please indicate appropriate region of the country for Plant & Material List. Region _____

POSTAGE AND HANDLING *SIGNATURE IS REQUIRED FOR ALL DELIVERIES.*	1–3 sets	4+ sets
DELIVERY No CODs (Requires street address—No P.O. Boxes)		
•Regular Service (Allow 7–10 business days delivery)	❑ $20.00	❑ $25.00
•Priority (Allow 4–5 business days delivery)	❑ $25.00	❑ $35.00
•Express (Allow 3 business days delivery)	❑ $35.00	❑ $45.00
OVERSEAS DELIVERY	fax, phone or mail for quote	

Note: All delivery times are from date Blueprint Package is shipped.

POSTAGE (From box above) $_____
SUBTOTAL $_____
SALES TAX (AZ & MI residents, please add appropriate state and local sales tax.) $_____
TOTAL (Subtotal and tax) $_____

YOUR ADDRESS (please print legibly)

Name _____

Street_____

City _____State_____Zip _____

Daytime telephone number (required) (_____) _____

* Fax number (required for reproducible orders) _____

TeleCheck® Checks By Phone℠ available

FOR CREDIT CARD ORDERS ONLY

Credit card number _____ Exp. Date: (M/Y) _____

Check one ❑ Visa ❑ MasterCard ❑ American Express

Order Form Key
HPT74

Signature (required) _____

Please check appropriate box: ❑ Licensed Builder-Contractor ❑ Homeowner

ORDER TOLL FREE!
1-800-521-6797

BY FAX: Copy the order form above and send it on our FAXLINE: 1-800-224-6699 OR 520-544-3086

1 BIGGEST & BEST

1001 of our best-selling plans in one volume. 1,074 to 7,275 square feet. 704 pgs $12.95 1K1

2 ONE-STORY

450 designs for all lifestyles. 800 to 4,900 square feet. 384 pgs $9.95 OS

3 MORE ONE-STORY

475 superb one-level plans from 800 to 5,000 square feet. 448 pgs $9.95 MO2

4 TWO-STORY

443 designs for one-and-a-half and two stories. 1,500 to 6,000 square feet. 448 pgs $9.95 TS

5 VACATION

430 designs for recreation, retirement and leisure. 448 pgs $9.95 VS3

6 HILLSIDE

208 designs for split-levels, bi-levels, multi-levels and walkouts. 224 pgs $9.95 HH

7 FARMHOUSE

300 Fresh Designs from Classic to Modern. 320 pgs. $10.95 FCP

8 COUNTRY HOUSES

208 unique home plans that combine traditional style and modern livability. 224 pgs $9.95 CN

9 BUDGET-SMART

200 efficient plans from 7 top designers, that you can really afford to build! 224 pgs $8.95 BS

10 BARRIER-FREE

Over 1,700 products and 51 plans for accessible living. 128 pgs $15.95 UH

11 ENCYCLOPEDIA

500 exceptional plans for all styles and budgets—the best book of its kind! 528 pgs $9.95 ENC

12 ENCYCLOPEDIA II

500 completely new plans. Spacious and stylish designs for every budget and taste. 352 pgs $9.95 E2

13 AFFORDABLE

300 Modest plans for savvy homebuyers. 256 pgs. $9.95 AH2

14 VICTORIAN

210 striking Victorian and Farmhouse designs from today's top designers. 224 pgs $15.95 VDH2

15 ESTATE

Dream big! Eighteen designers showcase their biggest and best plans. 224 pgs $16.95 EDH3

16 LUXURY

170 lavish designs, over 50% brand-new plans added to a most elegant collection. 192 pgs $12.95 LD3

17 EUROPEAN STYLES

200 homes with a unique flair of the Old World. 224 pgs $15.95 EURO

18 COUNTRY CLASSICS

Donald Gardner's 101 best Country and Traditional home plans. 192 pgs $17.95 DAG

19 COUNTRY

85 Charming Designs from American Home Gallery. 160 pgs. $17.95 CTY

20 TRADITIONAL

85 timeless designs from the Design Traditions Library. 160 pgs. $17.95 TRA

21 COTTAGES

245 Delightful retreats from 825 to 3,500 square feet. 256 pgs. $10.95 COOL

22 CABINS TO VILLAS

Enchanting Homes for Mountain Sea or Sun, from the Sater collection. 144 pgs $19.95 CCV

23 CONTEMPORARY

The most complete and imaginative collection of contemporary designs available anywhere. 256 pgs. $10.95 CM2

24 FRENCH COUNTRY

Live every day in the French countryside using these plans, landscapes and interiors. 192 pgs. $14.95 PN

25 SOUTHERN

207 homes rich in Southern styling and comfort. 240 pgs $8.95 SH

26 SOUTHWESTERN

138 designs that capture the spirit of the Southwest. 144 pgs $10.95 SW

27 SHINGLE-STYLE

155 Home plans from Classic Colonials to Breezy Bungalows. 192 pgs. $12.95 SNG

28 NEIGHBORHOOD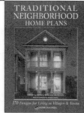

170 designs with the feel of main street America. 192 pgs $12.95 TND

29 CRAFTSMAN

170 Home plans in the Craftsman and Bungalow style. 192 pgs $12.95 CC

30 GRAND VISTAS

200 Homes with a View. 224 pgs $10.95 GV

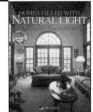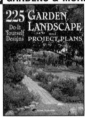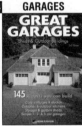
223

FOR FASTER SERVICE ORDER ONLINE AT
www.hwspecials.com

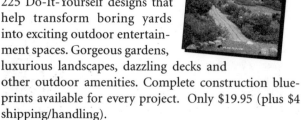